THE

WAR

ON

CHRISTIANS

By
Will Clark

The War On Christians

Copyright © 2014 by Will Clark

ISBN 13: 978-1502471987
ISBN 10: 1502471981

Published by
Motivation Basics
P.O. Box 6327
Diamondhead, MS 39525
Will01@aol.com

QUOTE

"A nation can survive its fools, and even the ambitious. But it cannot survive treason from within. An enemy at the gates is less formidable, for he is known and carries his banner openly. But the traitor moves amongst those within the gate freely, his sly whispers rustling through all the alleys, heard in the very halls of government itself. For the traitor appears not a traitor; he speaks in accents familiar to his victims, and he wears their face and their arguments, he appeals to the baseness that lies deep in the hearts of all men. He rots the soul of a nation, he works secretly and unknown in the night to undermine the pillars of the city, he infects the body politic so that it can no longer resist. A murderer is less to fear. The traitor is the plague." *Marcus Tullius Cicero, 58 B.C. Speech in the Roman Senate*

Contents

Introduction

Is there a war on Christianity? Although many who fervently support our current government's promises of ideological socialist concepts such as: share the wealth, fair share, social justice, and the bad millionaires and billionaires argue there is no war against Christians, Christianity, and God. However, simple research and understanding gives overwhelming evidence and examples there is a planned and purposeful attack on Christianity. There are two very definitive purposes for this war.

The roots of the war go deep, and its foundation has been specifically planned. There is a war, and the war is great. This article from the Jeremiahproject.com gives a broad overview of the war's strategies and tactics. The remainder of this book explains more specific areas and conditions.

From: Jeremiahproject.com - article titled: War on Christianity. The article begins:

"Jesus warned his disciples and explained why there exists a hatred for Christianity.

"If the world hates you, keep in mind that it hated me first. If you belonged to the world, it would love you as its own. As it is, you do not belong to the world, but I have chosen you out of the world. That is why the world hates you.

Remember the words I spoke to you: 'No servant is greater than his master.' If they persecuted me, they will persecute you also. If they obeyed my teaching, they will obey yours also. They will treat you this way because of my name, for they do not know the One who sent me. If I had not come and spoken to them, they would not be guilty of sin. Now, however, they have no excuse for their sin. He who hates me hates my Father as well. If I had not done among them what no one else did, they would not be guilty of sin. But now they have seen these miracles, and yet they have hated both me and my Father. But this is to fulfill what is written in their Law: 'They hated me without reason.' - John 15:18-25

What Christians are experiencing in the world today is not so much a "war on Christianity" as it is rebellion against God, and thus a hatred toward anything that points to God or His Son Jesus... and by extension a hatred of Christ's followers.

In recent decades, we have seen worldwide an escalating of this hatred of Christianity in the form of militant radical Islam. While this Islamic jihad has been exploding for years throughout the Middle East and Europe, it burst on the scene in America on September 11, 2001.

Many Islamic-dominated nations have adopted a fanatical, militant doctrine of persecution against all "infidels."

Close U.S. ally, Saudi Arabia has no religious freedom, all citizens must adhere to Sunni Islam. Others are imprisoned, tortured, detained, etc. for engaging in other religious activities. Apostasy is punishable by death. There are no public worship services for non-Muslims. Anyone who does mission work or converts Muslims faces expulsion, jail, or execution.

Since the September 11, 2001 attacks on the United States where 15 of the 19 hijackers were citizens of Saudi Arabia, the Saudi government has failed to implement a number of promised reforms related to promoting freedom of thought, conscience, and religion or belief. The Saudi government persists in banning all forms of public religious expression other than that of the government's own interpretation of one school of Sunni Islam; prohibits churches, synagogues, temples, and other non-Muslim places of worship; uses in its schools and posts online state textbooks that continue to espouse intolerance and incite violence; and periodically interferes with private religious practice.

The militant Islamic Government of Sudan severely restricts religious practice of all other types of religion and their restrictive Shari'ah law (Islamic law) attacks and threatens the Christian community. They are waging a self-described religious war against Christian, non-Muslim, and moderate Muslim persons by using torture, starvation, enslavement, and murder. They have violations of apostasy that could ultimately end up in the death penalty.

In Egypt (where the U.S. supported Arab Spring erupted that led to the overthrow of Hosni Mubarak), there continues to be serious problems of discrimination, intolerance, and other violations against religious minorities. Military and security forces are known to use excessive force and live ammunition targeting Coptic Christian demonstrators and places of worship resulting in dozens of deaths and hundreds of injuries. The government also continues to prosecute, convict, and imprison Egyptian citizens charged with blasphemy.

In U.S. occupied Afghanistan, the constitution and other laws and policies restrict religious freedom and, in practice the government generally enforced legal restrictions. Non-Muslim minority groups, particularly Christians, Hindus, and Sikhs, continue to be targets of persecution and discrimination. Shia and Sunni Islamic clergy, as well as many citizens, interpreted conversion from Islam as contravening the tenets of Islam. Conversion, considered an act of apostasy and a crime against Islam, could be punishable by death if the convert did not recant.

In Iraq, the government continues to tolerate systematic, ongoing, and egregious religious freedom violations. Religious sites and worshipers are targeted in violent attacks, often with impunity, and businesses viewed as "un - Islamic" are vandalized.

In Pakistan, the government has declared those that who "insult" Mohammed will be put to death. In Communist Laos more than 250 pastors and Christian workers have been arrested; more than 60 churches and Christian institutions have been shut down; and the government has forced many thousands of believers to sign documents to "renounce" their faith and belief in Christianity.

Other offenders of religious freedom according to the United States Commission on International Religious Freedom also include Burma,

China, Egypt, Eritrea, Iran, Nigeria, North Korea, Pakistan, Tajikistan, Turkey, Turkmenistan, Uzbekistan, and Vietnam. The CPC watch list of countries considered borderline and many eventually end up with aggressive religious persecution include: Belarus, Cuba, India, Indonesia, Laos, Russia, Somalia, and Venezuela.

In more than 40 nations around the world, people are being persecuted simply because of their faith. Hundreds of men and women are in prison serving sentences that range from a few months to life. They are not criminals who have robbed or murdered other citizens but Christians who were put on trial for their faith in Christ and found guilty. Christians are beaten, tortured, imprisoned, and murdered by those who are hostile to their faith in Jesus Christ.

'The Third Jihad: Radical Islam's Vision for America.' The Third Jihad is an in-depth documentary film that exposes the war the media is not telling you about. It reveals the enemy our government is too afraid to name.

As strange as it might sound, the U.S. created the enemies that attacked America on 9-11.

'The Third Jihad: Why Is The U.S. Supporting Al Qaeda In Syria?' The U.S. government trained, armed, funded and supported Osama bin Laden and his followers in Afghanistan. Zbigniew Brzezinski admitted that President Carter authorized the covert sponsorship of Muslim extremists, thus creating the mujahadeen and Al Qeada in Afghanistan in the 1980s to fight against Soviet aggression. In Afghanistan and then in Bosnia, the U.S. sponsored Muslim terror even as the State Department was officially condemning it.

In 2012, the Obama administration Secretary of State Hillary Rodham Clinton approved $1.3 billion in military aid in the form of F-16 fighter jets, M1 tanks, and similar weaponry to the Muslim Brotherhood in Egypt. Senator Rand Paul said, "I think it is a blunder of the first proportion to send sophisticated weapons to a country that allowed a mob to attack our embassy and to burn our flag. I find it objectionable to send weapons, F-16s and tanks to a country that allowed a mob chanting 'death to America' to threaten our American diplomats." Paul also stated that "these weapons threaten Israel's security" and "someday may be used against Israel."

The United States has also been supporting al Qeada affiliates in the Libyan civil war and Syrian civil war. While the Obama Administration has been very open about their support for the rebels, they apparently went to great lengths to cover up the arms shipments to al Qeada groups in Syria when it issued stand down orders to prevent the murders of four American citizens, including Ambassador Christopher Stevens in it's Benghazi consulate. The New York Times reported that since early 2012, the CIA has been aiding Arab governments and Turkey in obtaining and shipping weapons to the Syrian rebels. Days after the Benghazi attack that killed U.S. Ambassador Christopher Stevens, WND broke the story that Stevens himself played a central role in recruiting jihadists to fight Assad's regime in Syria, according to Egyptian and other Middle Eastern security officials.

During an interview with CNBC's Larry Kudlow, radio talk show host John Baxter said "Benghazi is not about Libya, Benghazi is about the policy of the Obama administration to involve the United States without clarity to the American people, not only in Libya but throughout the whole of the Arab world now in turmoil," Baxter told Kudlow. "Benghazi is about the NSC directing an operation that is perhaps shadowy, perhaps has a presidential finding, perhaps doesn't, that takes arms and men and puts them into Syria in the guise of the Free Syria Army."

Paul Mulshine of The Star Ledger asks, "Do you support the call by John McCain and Lindsey Graham for the U.S. to intervene on the side of the rebels in Syria? Congratulations! You're on the same side as the Muslim Brotherhood and Al Qaeda." The Muslim Brotherhood has been trying to overthrow the Assad regime since 1982 and joined with Al Qaeda to put together such operations as the Sept. 11 attack on New York. And now they're trying to take over Syria with the support of the United States.

Senator Rand Paul said of McCain's visit with Syrian rebels, "People say, 'Assad is such a bad guy.' He is. But on the other side we have alQaeda and now Nusra. So there's two ironies you have to overcome if you want to get involved in a war in Syria," he continued. "The first irony is you will be allied with al Qaeda. The second irony is most of the Christians are on the other side, so you may be arming Islamic rebels who may well be killing Christians. Does that make Assad a good person? No. I don't think there are any good people in this war, and there are some tragically innocent people who are going to be caught in the middle. But I just don't know that arming one side is going to make the tragedy any less."

Never before in American history have Christians experienced being

13

hated for following Jesus Christ as they are today.

While the war on Christianity in America and persecution of Christians has not yet reached the feverish pitch of persecution as it has in other parts of the world, there is a battle being waged and the Antichrist forces are making progress. Executive orders have been signed by our President, labor camps have been setup, our government has stockpiled guns and ammo, and Christians have been put on the terrorist list. It would seem we are getting close to the day that here in American we will suffer extreme persecution. (Note: more information about stockpiling ammunition at the end of chapter 9.)

Currently, there is still a Constitution in America that protects Christians and allows them to freely practice their faith. But, broiling beneath the surface, the same hatred of God that exists in other parts of the world is festering in all our institutions. Slowly, methodically, and incrementally the anti-God forces are working to remove that Constitutional barrier and replace it with the 10 Planks of Communism.

Forces within our government even use the so-called "war on terror" as a mechanism to actually support the enemies of our freedom. Following the 9/11 attacks, the U.S. Government has instituted numerous laws and regulations that strip Americans of the Constitutional rights and in some cases even paint Bible believing Christians as terrorists.

"But know this, that in the last days perilous times will come: For men will be lovers of themselves, lovers of money, boasters, proud, blasphemers, disobedient to parents, unthankful, unholy, unloving, unforgiving, slanderers, without self-control, brutal, despisers of good, traitors, headstrong, haughty, lovers of pleasure rather than lovers of God.... And from such people turn away!

...all who desire to live godly in Christ Jesus will suffer persecution. But evil men and impostors will grow worse and worse, deceiving and being deceived. But you must continue in the things which you have learned ..." 2 Timothy 3:1-5, 12-14

It is important to recognize that those engaged in the war on Christianity, working for the dissolution of our society and breakdown of the family have a spiritual agenda. They are not merely attempting to dismantle the historic cultural values of this nation and move us toward a new world order. They also want to destroy Christianity and Bible-based religion. It is a clear part of their agenda, and they have already moved a long way in that direction.

"Then you will be handed over to be persecuted and put to death, and you will be hated by all nations because of me." - Matt. 24:9

It was prophesied 2,000 years ago that Christians will be hated and ultimately handed over to be persecuted and put to death. The fulfillment of this prophecy began soon after Christ said it. Stephen was stoned (Acts 7:59); James was killed by Herod (Acts 12:2); and, the persecution under Nero took place before the destruction of Jerusalem, in which were put to death, with many others, Peter and Paul. Most of the apostles, it is believed, died by persecution. This prophecy was fulfilled then, and has been in all ages since.

Modern day Christians continue to witness the fulfillment of this prophecy even today. God hating zealots include people like David Rockefeller, Henry Kissinger, Zbigniew Brzezinsky, and the other politicos, European Royalty, world bankers and CEO's of multinational corporations who are members of the Council on Foreign Relations, the Bilderberg group and the Trilateral Commission. Their stated plan is to have a one world government which is opposed to God and Christ.

Secularism

In America it is called 'secularism' and is becoming visible in all walks of life and in all our institutions. Numerous legislative and legal battles which I'll discuss below attest to the fact that religious warfare is taking place.

The Media

Our entertainment industry and the news media sneer at anyone who defends Jesus Christ in public and have been leading a propaganda war of stereotyping Christians into a subordinate class. Their distortions reflect a genuine misunderstanding of who Christians are and what they believe.

Americas' mainstream news media ignores conservative and Christian news events, except when coverage makes religious leaders look "cold, intolerant and oppressive," says Washington, D.C.'s Media Research Center. Their coverage of the anti-Christian agenda is all but ignored and rarely reported on. Of course, that is understandable when you realize they are part of the anti-christian cabal and have agreed not to cover what is discussed at the globalist meetings they attend .

Though most Americans believe in God and regularly attend religious services, "religion and religious issues are hardly ever mentioned, much less covered, on network television morning, evening and magazine shows," said the center's chairman Brent Bozell. He said that the center has surveyed more than 18,000 nightly news shows broadcast by ABC, CBS, NBC, the Cable News Network and the Public Broadcasting Service, but found only 212 stories that focused on religion. That amounts to 1 percent of coverage although 52 percent of Americans say they attend church and more than 90 percent say that they pray regularly.

Network coverage of abortion and homosexuality "are never done from the religious viewpoint," Bozell said. Instead, "religious figures are regularly portrayed as reactionary roadblocks while their positive influences are rarely covered." Except at Christmastime, when the networks traditionally broadcast "heartwarming" segments in their broadcasts, the news shows usually portray religious groups and their leaders "as cold, intolerant and oppressive," Bozell said. ("TV news broadcasters unfair to Christians, says research center," Christian Crusade, April 1994)

Government
The federal government abridges the free exercise of religion in America by:

1. Regulating churches and other religious organizations through its tax laws.

In 2013, the IRS admitted to targeting conservative and Christian groups for greater scrutiny.

Among the organizations the IRS investigated and audited were the Billy Graham Evangelistic Association (BGEA) and the 180-year-old Baptist newspaper the Biblical Recorder, published by the North Carolina Baptist State Convention. The IRS reportedly also targeted the humanitarian relief group Samaritan's Purse. Both it and the BGEA are run by Franklin Graham, son of famed evangelical preacher Billy Graham.

The Washington Examiner reported that the IRS refused to approve an application of tax exempt status for a group called the Coalition for Life of Iowa unless it sent a letter certifying that it would not picket against Planned Parenthood. In addition, the Coalition was asked by the IRS about the content of its prayers.

The Weekly Standard reported that Lois Lerner, director of the IRS's Exempt Organizations Division, was accused of politically motivated harassment after a huge investigation into the Christian Coalition in the 1990s.

2. Limiting religious liberty in the area of public and private education.

3. Forbidding non-denominational prayer in public schools and at educational ceremonies.

4. Excluding the Bible from school classrooms and from other school property.

5. Refusing to permit the religious displays on public property, such as Christmas and Chanukah.

Navy Lt. Gordon James Klingenschmitt was punished by a commander for offering sectarian prayers at a memorial service for a fallen sailor.

Schools
Possibly the most sinister battlefield in the war on Christianity takes place in the classroom. The Ten Commandments have been prohibited on school bulletin boards and most forms of prayer have been declared unconstitutional in the nation's schools, even that which is student initiated.

Atheists and others who hate God despise Christians who help others come to a saving knowledge of Christ. They are determined to battle those who would help immature Christians -- particularly Christian children -- grow in their relationship with Jesus Christ.

Increasingly, our children are discriminated against for trying to present their Christian convictions in school.

In 1997 U.S. District Court Judge Ira DeMent struck down a law that required schools to allow voluntary student-initiated prayers at school events, saying it created excessive state entanglement in religion. He ordered the end to school-sponsored religious activities, such as prayers during morning announcements and at school events even though it isn't forced on students.

A high school student in Florida was suspended for handing out religious literature before and after - but not during - school hours. Two high school students in Texas were told by their principal they could not wear rosaries. The Principal claimed that they were symbols of gang activity, even though the boys were not involved in any gang.

In 2002, music teachers in Michigan, Maryland, and Virginia didn't allow students to perform traditional carols like "Silent Night" and "The First Noel" during Christmas. A New Jersey public school banned the Charles Dickens play, "A Christmas Carol" because of its spiritual overtones and message of redemption.

The Courts
1. Anthony Kennedy writing for the majority in U.S. v. Windsor (which declared the Defense of Marriage Act (DOMA) unconstitutional), Supreme Court Justice Anthony Kennedy wrote a anti-christian polemic disguised as a legal opinion attacking the Christian concept of marriage saying that those who stand up for traditional marriage, i.e. Christians, have an animus against gays, want to deny them equal dignity, want to brand them as unworthy, and have a hateful desire to harm a politically unpopular group. This God hating, pagan judge essentially branded Christians as a hate group, opening the door for future oppression by the courts. Apparently, Justice Kennedy perceives himself or at least the Court to be God with supremacy over the people in violation of the religious freedom and liberty guaranteed by the Constitution.

Declaration of Independence. 'Our rights come from God, not government.' Our Founders enshrined that notion in the Declaration of Independence saying, "We hold these truths to be self-evident, that all men are created equal, that they are endowed by their Creator with certain unalienable Rights, that among these are Life, Liberty and the pursuit of Happiness." Justice Kennedy is NOT the law giver God and the other justices are not on the bench to take away those rights "endowed by their Creator" while granting new laws and rights not envisioned by the Founders or the American people. In fact, the purpose of government, including the Judicial Branch, are addressed in the next sentence of the Declaration, "That to secure these rights, Governments are instituted among Men, deriving their just powers from the consent of the governed." We the people "consent" to the powers of Justice Kennedy and others to "secure these rights," not take them away. Perhaps it's time We the People withdraw our consent from those working to dissolve our Constitution and failing to secure the rights given us by God. Not coincidentally, the Declaration also addresses that issue in it's next sentence, "That whenever any Form of Government becomes destructive of these ends, it is the Right of the People to alter or to abolish it, and to institute new Government, laying its foundation on such principles and organizing its powers in such form, as to them shall seem most likely to effect their Safety and Happiness."

2. Judge Roy Moore in Gadsden, Alabama, was ordered to stop conducting prayers in his courtroom and displaying the Ten Commandments. That led Alabama Gov. Fob James, a supporter of prayer in public schools, to vow to use state troopers, if necessary, to allow Moore to continue the prayers.

3. Confessed child rapist James Arnett's sentence was overturned by an Ohio appeals court. The reason: the judge in his case quoted from Matthew 18:5-6 during sentencing.

The Public Square
The secularist trend in the public forum is to replace the word "Christmas" with "Season's Greetings" or "Happy Holidays."

In March 1998, The ACLU put pressure on the small town of Republic, Missouri to remove a fish symbol from its official logo, calling it a "secret sign of Christianity."

In April 1998, Rev. Patrick Mahoney was arrested for praying on the steps of the Supreme Court.

Tourists visiting Washington D.C. in 1997 were ordered by the police to stop praying in the rotunda of the U.S. Capitol.

In 2003, the National Park Service removed 30 year-old plaques inscribed with Bible verses at Grand Canyon following complaints from the American Civil Liberties Union.

The Workplace
The anti-Christian bias is a reality in many companies today -- as you will discover if you refuse to work on Sundays, if you question "shading the truth" in presentations, or if you stubbornly hold to your Christian standards.

A Christian employee of Hewlet Packard was fired for posting Bible verses condemning homosexual behavior on his desk in response to posters displayed during a company campaign to promote a diverse work force. (WorldNetDaily)

Businesses
1. Even though Krispy Kreme promises to give students a free doughnut for each "A" on their report cards, a store in Schereville, Indiana refused to reward the Kamp children for A's received in Bible classes. ["Chain Won't Give a Doughnut for an 'A' in Bible", Wendy

Cloyd, Assistant Editor, CitizenLink]

2. David and Barbara Green: The devout Christian Hobby Lobby owners, David and Barbara Green, only want to live the American dream and to be free to do business according to their beliefs. They seek to honor God in their business by "operating their company in a manner consistent with Biblical principles."

But, HHS secretary Kathleen Sebelius and the Obama administration thinks otherwise. The Oklahoma-based Hobby Lobby company sued the Obama administration in September 2012 regarding the U.S. Department of Health and Human Services' abortion-pill mandate, a regulation under the Affordable Care Act (aka Obamacare), requiring the chains to offer potential abortion-inducing drugs in their employee health-care plans.

The U.S. Supreme Court announced in Nov. 2013, it will take up Sebelius v. Hobby Lobby Stores, Inc. case addressing the Constitutionally guaranteed rights of business owners to operate their family companies without violating their deeply held religious convictions.

This case has ramifications far beyond abortifacients such as the morning after pill. The pagan mandates in Obamacare also include sterilizations and sex change operations. If this law is allowed to stand, the legal precedent will be set for these kind of immoral practices to explode along with other even more evil practices.

Steve Deace said on his radio program there is a danger here with the Supreme Court hearing this case. If the Court says the Christians at

Hobby Lobby do not have to do what their pagan government told them to do because they have a First Amendment right to object, then you have all kinds of rights to object to being compelled to participate in all kinds of immorality that the government wants you to accept. If the Court rules for Hobby Lobby here, it will severely undercut it's own landmark ruling in the DOMA case. Given the Court's recent history, I wouldn't expect them to defend Christian religious freedom.

Michael Peroutka of the Institute on the Constitution points out that the centralized government is exerting itself to be God and to force it's brand of morality on the people rather than seeing itself as the agent supposed to protect those rights given by God and guaranteed by the Constitution.

Christians Standing United

All men will hate you because of me, but he who stands firm to the end will be saved. - Matt. 10:22

Like-minded Christians should be standing firm together in our struggles while supporting and loving one another (John 15:17; Rom. 12:9-13). Instead of cooperating with unbelievers, we should "shake the dust off your feet when you leave that home or town." (Matt. 10:14) We should refuse any further connection with them.

You adulterous people, don't you know that friendship with the world is hatred toward God? Anyone who chooses to be a friend of the world becomes an enemy of God. - James 4:4

Turn OFF that ungodly television, stop going to their theaters, defy the governments unjust laws, stand in contempt in their corrupt courtrooms, stop voting for their corrupt politicians and demand government to return to just weights and measures, remove your children from their secular humanist public schools, fire your MD and stop using those drug pushers to attend to your health, free yourself from the slavery of employment if you're working for an ungodly company, boycott the products of ungodly businesses and multi-national corporations and instead support those products and services of fellow believers. Read A Christian Patriot Action Plan to Resist the New World Order for a more complete manifesto of patriotic Christian activism. And, instead of being intimidated in the public square, Christians should be flooding that arena with the message, "The kingdom of heaven is near." (Matt. 10:7)

Do not conform any longer to the pattern of this world, but be transformed by the renewing of your mind. - Romans 12:2

Instead of conforming to this world, true Christians are called to be different. Christians should be doing everything possible to get off the worlds' grid. In addition to the things above a Christian can do, I would also suggest a renewal of your mind from the godless propaganda that has distorted your beliefs of just about everything. Learn the truth about the people, places, and things that have been influencing your life and the Antichrist will ultimately use to deceive even the elect (Matt. 24:24). Wake Up!

No man can serve two masters: for either he will hate the one, and love the other; or else he will hold to the one, and despise the other. Ye cannot serve God and mammon. - Matt. 6:24 (KJV)

I am not suggesting the above actions from a reconstructionist theology point of view. I certainly don't expect Christians are going to change the world into some heavenly utopia. You and I are not going to save the world. We can, however, influence some individuals and help them find the saving grace of God. And, I believe we are each individually responsible for our own choices of whom we serve. My prayer for you and I is that we come to the end of our time and hear, "Well done, good and faithful servant; thou hast been faithful over a few things, I will make thee ruler over many things: enter thou into the joy of thy lord." (Matt. 25:23, KJV)
End of article.

Chapter 1

Is There a War On Christians?

Is there really a war against Christianity? Many adamantly argue there is not a war against Christianity, Christians, and God; and blame this idea as ideological and political positioning. A recent example is expressed in the following article: 'Charles Blow's self-defeating column against Christianity' By Denny Burk on January 4, 2014 in Christianity, Politics:

"In his most recent column for The New York Times, Charles Blow argues that the Republican Party is manipulating the benighted convictions of Christians for political purposes. Blow accuses the GOP of manufacturing a war on Christians in a cynical attempt to keep its base riled up for the next election.

In short, Blow says that there are no real threats to religious freedom in this country. It's all just a figment of our imaginations. It's a ruse designed by the GOP to ensconce Christians in their most "base convictions" (like belief in the biblical creation account and the

Bible's definition of marriage). If it weren't for the GOP manipulating the base, perhaps Christians would eventually get over some of their superstitious and unfounded beliefs.

There is so much wrong with Blow's article that it's difficult to know where to start. But perhaps I should point out the fundamental self-defeating contradiction at the heart of it. Blow argues that the "war" on Christians is a lie. There really isn't any threat at all for Christians to be concerned about. Then he spends the rest of his article in a sustained assault on Christianity. He castigates Christians ignorant enough to believe that God created the world apart from evolutionary processes. He looks down his nose at Christians who are so unenlightened as to believe what the Bible teaches about marriage. And then there is this condescending line:

'I don't personally have a problem with religious faith, even in the extreme, as long as it doesn't supersede science and it's not used to impose outdated mores on others.'

In other words, Blow has no problem with Christianity as long as it never contradicts the spirit of the age and never makes claims of any public consequence—which is another way of saying, "I have no problem with Christianity so long as it ceases to be Christian."

Blow can't have it both ways. He cannot deny the existence of a "war" on Christianity while simultaneously waging that war himself. Not only is he waging that war. He's doing so in the most strident terms possible–the kinds of arguments that form the basis for real assaults on religious freedom. To wit, he alleges a strong correlation between religious conviction and "poor societal conditions." He even goes so far as to say that convictional Christians stand against "common sense and the common good." Ideologically, this a mere step away from the way the Romans regarded the Christians they persecuted–as "enemies of the human race."

It is astonishing that Blow can be so unaware of the contradiction at the heart of his argument. He denies the existence of secular antipathy towards Christians, and yet he himself is the embodiment of it in this column. If you want to see evidence that there really is a growing intolerance of biblical Christianity among secular elites, read Blow's column. Unless Blow is an imaginary man, this is not just a figment of our imaginations." End.

This is another example of belittling or discrediting the idea there is a real and serious war against Christians. It's an article posted on huffingtonpost.com by Roy Speckhardt on 7-31-2014. Speckhardt is Executive Director, American Humanist Association:

When Newt Gingrich, the former speaker of the House, was asked how LGBTQ couples could form a meaningful relationship in a country often hostile to gay people, he responded without a sense of irony that "The bigotry question goes both ways. And there is a lot more anti-Christian bigotry today than there is on the other side."

Hearing elected officials alleging U.S. based Christian persecution is surprisingly common given the prominent position of Christianity in all walks of American life. It used to be that just the unelected extreme religious right that would use the tactic of pretending the majority was an embattled underdog. The early darling of ultra-conservative Christianity, Ralph Reed, was famous for saying in 1991: "I do guerrilla warfare ... I paint my face and travel at night. You don't know it's over until you're in a body bag. You don't know until election night." But it seemed that despite the Christian Coalition's departure from the political scene, Reed and others were ultimately successful as their ideological colleagues now walk the halls of Congress. With the blaring megaphones of politicians, they assert false claims of a U.S. "War on Christianity."

Failed GOP presidential candidate Rick Santorum may be the right-wing champion in the War on Christianity. Santorum believes Christians are fighting a war against extinction, referring constantly to what Ronald Reagan said in his 1967 California governor's inaugural address, "Freedom is a fragile thing and is never more than one generation away from extinction." Santorum points to his own claim that Christians discriminating against those in the LGBT community will be forced into re-education camps as "proof" of Christian persecution and part of this war on Christianity. Santorum's fervor is so intense that his film company, EchoLight Studios, will soon release One Generation Away: the Erosion of Religious Liberty - a documentary-style film focusing on the disintegration of religious freedom across the country.

According to Right Wing Watch, Texas Representative Louie Gohmert made a statement that President Obama and his administration has "gone to war with Christianity" because, according to Gohmert, "you can't practice what you believe... this administration will tell you what religious practices you can participate in and what you can't." And previous Republican Party nominee for Vice President, Sarah Palin spoke at Liberty University in December of 2013 saying, "Those who want to try to abort Christ from Christmas...

these are angry atheists armed with an attorney, they are not the majority of Americans..." Only in this supposed war against Christianity are attorneys considered artillery.

However popular the War on Christianity may seem, it is simply a fallacy in the United States. When it comes to holding office, since 1869 "every [American] president has been affiliated with a Christian church," whereas an atheist has never been president. A Pew survey conducted in 2013 revealed overwhelmingly that the American Public is still much more likely to vote for a Christian candidate as opposed to an atheist, and generally, as opposed to atheists, Americans feel more favorably towards Christians. Amidst all the talk of religious persecution, Christmas is still the only religious holiday that is federally recognized with a holiday. Political humorist Bill Maher pointed out that when Eric Cantor leaves after being booted from office, there will be "no non-Christian Republicans in Congress."

The truth is, Christianity is not under fire in the United States and it is ridiculous to think it is. Sarah Palin was right on one point, atheists are not the majority in this country, Christians are, and they are over-represented on Capitol Hill and in other positions of influence. There is no American war on Christianity and masquerading the fight for religious imposition as a fight to protect Christians from this fabricated war is offensive to those truly suffering prejudice and persecution. Fundamentalist Christians should stop subverting religious freedom for all by dropping the religious war metaphors and ceasing their efforts to use the power of government to impose their faith on others. End of article.

These two articles express the typical belief by many who challenge the reality of God and Jesus, or who are so adamant on the opposing political side that they reject God to serve their political ideologies that they blind themselves to the concept of Creation. Accepting the idea of creation would destroy their political idealism and, to them, would deny the concept of evolution. They reject the idea of that war to fulfill their earthly connections and ambitions.

So, the questions must be asked more seriously: Is there now a war against Christians? If so, who is waging this war and who are its leaders? Not only is there a war; this war was prophesied over two thousand years ago.

Yes, there is a clear and definitive war against Christians, and other related religions such as Jewish, and any other religion that recognizes and accepts God as identified in the Bible. This war was prophesied two thousand years ago by the Apostle John as he wrote the Book of Revelation while he was exiled on the island of Patmos. Patmos is still there in its same location just off the coast of Turkey. It's near the ancient city of Ephesus, one of the seven biblical churches, and the location where many of Jesus's disciples taught while that area was called 'Asia Minor.' Although cryptic, Chapter 12 in the Book of Revelation explains the beginning of this war on Christianity and its cause:

"And there appeared a great wonder in heaven; a woman clothed with the sun, and the moon under her feet, and upon her head a crown of twelve stars.
2. And she being with child cried, travailing in birth, and pained to be delivered.
3. And there appeared another wonder in heaven; and behold a great

red dragon, having seven heads and ten horns, and seven crowns upon his heads.

4. And his tail drew the third part of the stars of heaven, and did cast them to the earth: and the dragon stood before the woman which was ready to be delivered, for to devour her child as soon as it was born.

5. And she brought forth a man child, who was to rule all nations with a rod of iron:..

6. And the woman fled into the wilderness, where she hath a place prepared of God,...

7. And there was war in heaven: Michael and his angels fought against the dragon; and the dragon fought and his angels,

8. And prevailed not; neither was their place found any more in heaven.

9. And the great dragon was cast out, that old serpent, called the Devil, and Satan, which deceiveth the whole world: he was cast out into the earth, and his angels were cast out with him.

13. And when the dragon saw that he was cast unto the earth, he persecuted the woman which brought forth the man child.

14. And to the woman were given two wings of a great eagle, that she might fly into the wilderness, into her place, where she is nourished for a time, and times, and half a time, from the face of the serpent.

17. And the dragon was wroth with the woman, and went to make war with the remnant of her seed, which keep the commandments of God, and have the testimony of Jesus Christ."

A summary: The known world at that time, primarily Rome, knew the Jews were expecting a messiah even before Jesus was born. They waited for him, and at the expected time had all newborns killed hoping one would be that expected messiah. This mass killing is known as the 'Massacre of the Innocents,' by Herod the Great, the

Roman appointed King of the Jews. It included the execution of all young male children in the vicinity of Jerusalem. "upon her head a crown of twelve stars" likely refers to the twelve tribes of Jews at that time.

Verse 14 seems most cryptic until 'two wings of a great eagle' is understood. Jews and Christians were totally persecuted until a 'great eagle' suddenly adopted Christianity as the world religion. Constantine the 'Great' who ruled from 306-337 adopted Christianity after a vision he had in 312 that he attributed to helping him win a great battle against a major enemy. It was the Battle of Milvian Bridge.

According to writings, before the battle Constantine looked into the sun and saw a cross of light, with the words, "in this sign, conquer." He had his men paint a cross on their shields before the battle; that resulted in a major victory. As a result, he adopted Christianity for the Roman Empire. Soon afterwards, his mother, Saint Helen, made pilgrimage trips to the Holy Land identifying and preserving special Christian landmarks.

What about the 'two wings of a great eagle?' An eagle with two widespread wings was the standard symbol for the Roman Empire. It was proudly carried on a tall staff ahead of marching troops.

The prophesy about the continuing war on Christians today is very clear - and without doubt. Verse 17 is very specific and needs little interpretation: "And the dragon was wroth with the woman, and went to make war with the remnant of her seed, which keep the commandments of God, and have the testimony of Jesus Christ." This war continues even today, in every part of our American society and in most parts of the world. Modern-day Christians are the 'remnants of her seed,' as members of Christ's church. The 'woman' identified in this chapter includes the body of Christians - those who believe in God and Jesus Christ.

Chapter 12 gives a quick overview to describe the beginning of the war on Christianity. It also describes a brief respite after Christianity's acceptance by the powerful in the world at that time. That respite is with Constantine's formation of the Roman Catholic Church - which accepted and protected Christians against Roman atrocities which had been the previous Roman reaction to Christians.

Verse 17 explains that when that respite is over, that great war will reignite. The next chapter, 13, gives the modern-day description of the continuation of that war. The war continues against 'the remnant of her seed.' The world is now making a rapid transformation to that time.

This final war has already begun, and will accelerate when the world, the seven continents, are under one rule, or one authority. That likely will begin in the United Nations or under a stronger NATO. That body will select their leader and give him a title. Who knows what the title will be - perhaps president, chairman, or czar. In either case he's the one likely to transform into the 'beast.' Revelation describes him as the 'beast.' Other parts in the Bible describe him as the 'Antichrist' or the 'little horn.' What Biblical verse announces this transitional event? This is indicated by Revelation 13:1-2:

"And I stood upon the sand of the sea, and saw a beast rise up out of the sea, having seven heads and ten horns, and upon his horns ten crowns, and upon his heads the name of blasphemy.

2. And the beast which I saw was like unto a leopard, and his feet were as the feet of a bear, and his mouth as the mouth of a lion: and the dragon gave him his power, and his seat, and great authority."

The sea is mentioned many places in the Bible; however it doesn't actually mean a sea as in an ocean or a body of water. Many references incorporate another part that describes that sea as a large body of people. The significant part of the first verse is that John includes the word 'sand' to indicate an actual body of water - in this case the water of the earth from which the seven continents - the seven heads - rise.

Some interpret the 'seven heads' as the seven hills of Rome, suggesting the beast will emerge from Rome - or has already emerged from Rome in the form of Emperor Nero. Obviously, John included the word 'sand' to indicate from an actual body of water and not from seven hills on the same body of land. Some interpreters even suggest the 'seven heads' and the hills of Rome indicate even a Pope could become the beast. Understanding this body of water concept totally discredits this idea.

The ten horns and crowns are described as powerful countries and leaders by most interpreters. Each of those ten leaders will (blaspheme) deny or mock God. This would suggest they will continue - or lead - the war against Christianity after the world is under one rule.

Verse 2 is the one that explains the creation of the 'beast' or the

'Antichrist.' That's when "the dragon gives him his power, and his seat, and great authority." Until this time, the person who will become the Antichrist is not actually the Antichrist. He is the Antichrist in waiting - doing great things to make his followers adore and worship him. But what about the other descriptions of the leopard, bear and lion?

Since no other references or descriptions are given, the likely suggestion is to consider the strengths of each and compare to the newly-created beast. What are the strengths of each?

The leopard is a cat. All cats are stealthy - which perhaps could be considered 'deception.' The cat sneaks up on its prey and makes no sudden move of its intent until it's too late for the prey to escape its grasp. The beast does this by being deceptive; with deception he captures his unwary worshipers and followers until they are under his complete control, persuasion, and domination. As described in other places in the Bible, beginning with Genesis, he is a deceiver and a liar.

A bear has great strength. Another reference describes the beast as 'stout.' This means the beast has much power; which might indicate a powerful position that others must follow. Threats, intimidation, and retribution are powerful strengths when enforced by one who has much political and military power. He will likely be taller than most surrounding him. His presence will be conspicuous.

The lion is known not only for its strength and its stealthy cunning, but also for its great roar. Perhaps this analogy indicates the beast will have a great mouth and can speak well - with great persuasion. He will be heard, and his words will be very powerful and influential.

The beast will also be a great blasphemer who will deny and speak against God. Chapter 13 further describes the beast:

Verse 5, "And there was given unto him a mouth speaking great things and blasphemies;..." Verse 6, "And he opened his mouth in blasphemy against God, to blaspheme his name, and his tabernacle, and them that dwell in heaven."

Finally, Verse 7 describes his power to make war against Christians: "And it was given unto him to make war with the saints, and to overcome them; and power was given him over all kindreds, and tongues, and nations." In many places, especially in Revelation, the word 'saints' is used generally to express those who worship God - not necessarily one who has been proclaimed a 'Saint.' This verse also says his power against Christians will be world-wide with inclusion of the words, 'all nations.'

Is there really a world-wide war on Christians as clearly prophesied in the Bible? Absolutely and positively. There is too much evidence for even the most ardent disbeliever to deny. There is an insidious powerful war on Christians in every part of the world - including in our own great America where "In God we Trust."

This war against Christians, this growing hatred against God, was prophesied in other biblical scripture. Another clear definition and warning is explained in John 15: 18-25:

"If the world hate you, ye know that it hated me before it hated you.

If ye were of the world, the world would love his own: but because ye are not of the world, but I have chosen you out of the world, therefore the world hateth you. Remember the word that I said unto you, The servant is not greater than his lord. If they have persecuted me, they will also persecute you; if they have kept my saying, they will keep yours also.

But all these things will they do unto you for my name's sake, because they know not him that sent me. If I had not come and spoken unto them, they had not had sin; but now they have no cloak for their sin. He that hateth me hateth my Father also.

If I had not done among them the works which none other man did, they had not had sin; but now have they both seen and hated both me and my Father. But this cometh to pass, that the word might be fulfilled that is written in their law, They hated me without a cause."

This modern war against God and Christianity began creeping forward in America in the 1950s - 1970s with the emerging atheist movement. During the late 1940s until the 1950s most Americans still felt blessed with the hand of God carrying them safely through the Second World War. Americans led the way to preserve world freedom and hope; that hope being accepted as a special gift from God.

During this brief period, very few openly expressed a disbelief in God. When the few who did, they were frowned upon as having no respect for humanity. America was proudly a Christian nation. Our presidents and other senior leaders openly expressed our nation's belief in God and Jesus, and their guiding hands for our generous humanity and great prosperity.

This war was openly announced in America when Barack Obama forcefully proclaimed to a liberal Christian group in 2006, "We are no longer a Christian nation." Although he added in that speech after he said, "We are no longer a Christian nation - not just," the intent was very clear. His intention was to express that America would no longer be guided by Christian principles and concepts; those which had guided the formation and development of a great and Godly nation guided not only by biblical principles but also by humane principles of a caring society. Although these Christian principles had been slipping away from America for quite some time, his comments announced a new and more vicious assault on Christians. It was the verbal proclamation of the war John described when he wrote the Book of Revelation.

Did Barack Obama have a serious and determined background against Christianity when he made that statement, "We are no longer a Christian nation?" Perhaps this war had already been predetermined when he wrote in his book, 'Audacity of Hope': "I will stand with the Muslims should the political winds shift in an ugly direction."

The war against Christians became even more blatant and obvious when God was openly denied three times at the 2012 Democratic National Convention. By voice vote of the entire assembly, they rejected placing God's name in their party platform; many from the floor even booed and mocked the proposal. Perhaps this three times denied activity has another prophetic origin announcing the war against God and Christianity.

At the Lord's Supper, Jesus told Peter that he would deny Jesus three times before the rooster crowed. Jesus was arrested that night, and as he had said, Peter denied knowing Jesus three times before the rooster crowed. Jesus looked Peter in the eyes as the rooster crowed. Peter wept in an action titled, The Repentance of Peter.

Isn't it ironic and prophetic that God's name was denied three times at the 2012 Democratic National Convention? Not once, not twice, but three times the convention members, by voice vote, chose not to include God's name in the party platform. After the third vote, the chairman falsely claimed the vote had been two-thirds in the affirmative, and God's name and the recognition of Jerusalem were put back in the platform.

Was the prophesy by Jesus regarding Peter a hidden message about how God would be rejected at a later time? Was Peter used as an example to warn of humankind's modern-day denial of God? Why was God's name removed from the platform in the first place? What pressure, and from whom was someone forced to take that action? Only one man had enough power and authority to force that omission, and his blasphemy against God was exposed. That blasphemy continued on the convention floor and was tolerated by his followers. That prophetic rooster crowed over 2000 years ago.

This is the link to that latest three denials at the Democratic Convention. No roosters were crowing, but many in the audience were protesting when the chairman falsely claimed there were enough affirmative votes to put the reference to God and Jerusalem back in the Democratic platform:

http://www.youtube.com/watch?v=fAwlyYyiIS4

Nearly all Americans in our past worshiped God to give thanks for the creation of our country and for its great blessings. Through Obama's leadership and influence, God's name now has been cast out and unwelcome from many institutions in America. How far will these exclusions go; perhaps to the point of total exclusions and even persecution?

Does not evil and persecution left unchecked become more acceptable and normal; does it not often lead to tyranny? How can evil be recognized and judged in a society not influenced by the respect for God's creation? Will Obama's influence create a condition that one day will cause Christians and Jews to flee to the wilderness as they escape the Abomination of Desolation when the beast sits on the thrown in Jerusalem? Christians are now being attacked in every segment of our American society. The foundation of our society, and perhaps existence, is fast eroding. The 'War on Christianity' is a war on America. If Christianity falls, America falls with it.

There are three basic foundations of the War on Christianity. The first is to facilitate a program called 'Agenda 21.' Agenda 21 is explained in the next chapter.

Chapter 2

Agenda 21

Understanding the war; it's illusive because it's three pronged: direct Islamic attacks; the Third Jihad by the Muslim Brotherhood; an insidious attack to create a standard One-World Order as a socialist state through implementing Agenda 21.

Agenda 21 is a United Nations program giving guidelines for social development in the 21st century. It's also known as 'Sustainable Development.' Briefly, the program calls for one-world control over all land use in the world. Certain parcels would be designed for specific uses to support the one-world program. It also calls for a more equal distribution of wealth and resources worldwide, so that one community would be no more advanced than another community. Each community would be separated urban pods that would not require automobiles. The plan is for the urban pods to be so all-inclusive only bicycles would be needed.

What is Agenda 21? How does it influence the War against

Christians? It's described further in Wikipedia:

"Agenda 21 is a non-binding, voluntarily implemented action plan of the United Nations with regard to sustainable development. It is a product of the UN Conference on Environment and Development (UNCED) held in Rio de Janeiro, Brazil, in 1992. It is an action agenda for the UN, other multilateral organizations, and individual governments around the world that can be executed at local, national, and global levels. The "21" in Agenda 21 refers to the 21st Century. It has been affirmed and modified at subsequent UN conferences.

Structure and contents

Agenda 21 is a 300-page document divided into 40 chapters that have been grouped into 4 sections:

Section I: Social and Economic Dimensions is directed toward combating poverty, especially in developing countries, changing consumption patterns, promoting health, achieving a more sustainable population, and sustainable settlement in decision making.

Section II: Conservation and Management of Resources for Development includes atmospheric protection, combating deforestation, protecting fragile environments, conservation of biological diversity (biodiversity), control of pollution and the management of biotechnology, and radioactive wastes.

Section III: Strengthening the Role of Major Groups includes the roles of children and youth, women, NGOs (non-governmental organizations,) local authorities, business and industry, and workers;

and strengthening the role of indigenous peoples, their communities, and farmers.

Section IV: Means of Implementation; implementation includes science, technology transfer, education, international institutions and financial mechanisms.

Development and evolution

The full text of Agenda 21 was made public at the UN Conference on Environment and Development (Earth Summit), held in Rio de Janeiro on June 13, 1992, where 178 governments voted to adopt the program. The final text was the result of drafting, consultation, and negotiation, beginning in 1989 and culminating at the two-week conference.

In 1997, the UN General Assembly held a special session to appraise the status of Agenda 21. The Assembly recognized progress as "uneven" and identified key trends, including increasing globalization, widening inequalities in income, and continued deterioration of the global environment. A new General Assembly Resolution (S-19/2) promised further action.

Main article: World Summit on Sustainable Development

The Johannesburg Plan of Implementation, agreed at the World Summit on Sustainable Development (Earth Summit 2002) affirmed UN commitment to "full implementation" of Agenda 21, alongside achievement of the Millennium Development Goals and other international agreements.

Agenda 21 for culture (2002)
Main article: Agenda 21 for culture

The first World Public Meeting on Culture, held in Porto Alegre, Brazil, in 2002, came up with the idea to establish guidelines for local cultural policies, something comparable to what Agenda 21 was for the environment. They are to be included in various subsections of Agenda 21 and will be carried out through a wide range of sub-programs beginning with G8 countries.

Rio+20 (2012)
Main article: United Nations Conference on Sustainable Development

In 2012, at the United Nations Conference on Sustainable Development the attending members reaffirmed their commitment to Agenda 21 in their outcome document called "The Future We Want". 180 leaders from nations participated.

Implementation

The Commission on Sustainable Development acts as a high-level forum on sustainable development and has acted as preparatory committee for summits and sessions on the implementation of Agenda 21. The UN Division for Sustainable Development acts as the secretariat to the Commission and works "within the context of" Agenda 21. Implementation by member states remains voluntary, and its adoption has varied.

Local level:

The implementation of Agenda 21 was intended to involve action at international, national, regional and local levels. Some national and state governments have legislated or advised that local authorities take steps to implement the plan locally, as recommended in Chapter 28 of the document. These programs are often known as "Local Agenda 21" or "LA21". For example, in the Philippines, the plan is "Philippines Agenda 21" (PA21). The group, ICLEI-Local Governments for Sustainability, formed in 1990; today its members come from over 1,000 cities, towns, and counties in 88 countries and is widely regarded as a paragon of Agenda 21 implementation.

In other countries, opposition to Agenda 21's ideas has surfaced to varied extents. In some cases, opposition has been legislated into several States limiting or forbidding the participation and/or funding of local government activities that support Agenda 21.

Europe turned out to be the continent where LA21 was best accepted and most implemented. In Sweden, for example, all local governments have implemented a Local Agenda 21 initiative.

National level:

The UN Department of Economic and Social Affairs' Division for Sustainable Development monitors and evaluates progress, nation by nation, towards the adoption of Agenda 21, and makes these reports available to the public on its website.

Australia, for example, is a signatory to Agenda 21 and 88 of its municipalities subscribe to ICLEI, an organization that promotes Agenda 21 globally. Australia's membership is second only to that of the United States. European countries generally possess well documented Agenda 21 statuses. France, whose national government, along with 14 cities, is a signatory, boasts nationwide programs supporting Agenda 21. The French activist group Nouvelle Force announced in March 2012 that they viewed Agenda 21 as a "sham".

In Africa, national support for Agenda 21 is strong and most countries are signatories. But support is often closely tied to environmental challenges specific to each country; for example, in 2002 Sam Nujoma, who was then President of Namibia, spoke about the importance of adhering to Agenda 21 at the 2002 Earth Summit, noting that as a semi-arid country, Namibia sets a lot of store in the United Nations Convention to Combat Desertification (UNCCD). Furthermore, there is little mention of Agenda 21 at the local level in indigenous media.

Only major municipalities in sub-Saharan African countries are members of ICLEI. Agenda 21 participation in North African countries mirrors that of Middle Eastern countries, with most countries being signatories but little to no adoption on the local-government level. Countries in sub-Saharan Africa and North Africa generally have poorly documented Agenda 21 status reports. By contrast, South Africa's participation in Agenda 21 mirrors that of modern Europe, with 21 city members of ICLEI and support of Agenda 21 by national-level government.

Specific countries:

United States

The national focal point in the United States is the Division Chief for Sustainable Development and Multilateral Affairs, Office of Environmental Policy, Bureau of Oceans and International Environmental and Scientific Affairs, U.S. Department of State. A June 2012 poll of 1,300 United States voters by the American Planning Association found that 9% supported Agenda 21, 6% opposed it, and 85% thought they didn't have enough information to form an opinion.

The United States is a signatory country to Agenda 21, but because Agenda 21 is a legally non-binding statement of intent and not a treaty, the United States Senate was not required to hold a formal debate or vote on it. It is therefore not considered to be law under Article Six of the United States Constitution. President George Bush was one of the 178 heads of government who signed the final text of the agreement at the Earth Summit in 1992, and in the same year Representatives Nancy Pelosi, Eliot Engel and William Broomfield spoke in support of United States House of Representatives Concurrent Resolution 353, supporting implementation of Agenda 21 in the United States.

In the United States, over 528 cities are members of ICLEI, an international sustainability organization that helps to implement the Agenda 21 and Local Agenda 21 concepts across the world. The United States has nearly half of the ICLEI's global membership of 1,200 cities promoting sustainable development at a local level. The United States also has one of the most comprehensively documented Agenda 21 status reports. In response to the opposition, Don Knapp, U.S. spokesman for the ICLEI, has said "Sustainable development is not a top-down conspiracy from the U.N., but a bottom-up push from local governments".

The Arizona Chamber of Commerce and Industry successfully lobbied against an anti-sustainable development bill in 2012, arguing "It would be bad for business" as it could drive away corporations that have embraced sustainable development.

Opposition:

During the last decade, opposition to Agenda 21 has increased within the United States at the local, state, and federal levels. The Republican National Committee has adopted a resolution opposing Agenda 21, and the Republican Party platform stated that "We strongly reject the U.N. Agenda 21 as erosive of American sovereignty." Several state and local governments have considered or passed motions and legislation opposing Agenda 21. Alabama became the first state to prohibit government participation in Agenda 21. Many other states, including Arizona, are drafting, and close to passing legislation to ban Agenda 21.

Activists, some of whom have been associated with the Tea Party movement, (reported) by The New York Times and The Huffington Post, have said that Agenda 21 is a conspiracy by the United Nations to deprive individuals of property rights. Columnists in The Atlantic have linked opposition to Agenda 21 to the property rights movement in the United States." End of article.

This is another article by Beforeitsnews.com, July 10, 2013, regarding Agenda 21:

"...why has it caused concern world-wide? Is Agenda 21, also known as "sustainable development", really so evil that it has been described as: "a future in which people would be forced to live with five others in 20-by-20 living spaces with push-button furniture in high-rises across major cities. The complexes would serve three vegetarian meals a day, feature mosques and have a 24-7 on-call doctor to discuss taking one's own life."

What is Sustainable Development? According to its authors, the objective of sustainable development is to integrate economic, social and environmental policies in order to achieve reduced consumption, social equity, and the preservation and restoration of biodiversity. Sustainablists insist that every societal decision be based on environmental impact, focusing on three components; global land use, global education, and global population control and reduction.

(Social Equity - Social Justice - Explained in the next chapter.)

Social justice is described as the right and opportunity of all people "to benefit equally from the resources afforded us by society and the environment." Redistribution of wealth. Private property is a social injustice since not everyone can build wealth from it. National sovereignty is a social injustice. Universal health care is a social justice. All part of Agenda 21 policy.

Economic Prosperity

Public Private Partnerships (PPP). Special dealings between government and certain, chosen corporations which get tax breaks, grants and the government's power of Eminent Domain to implement sustainable policy. Government-sanctioned monopolies.

Local Sustainable Development policies

Smart Growth, Wildlands Project, Resilient Cities, Regional Visioning Projects, STAR Sustainable Communities, Green jobs, Green Building Codes, "Going Green," Alternative Energy, Local Visioning, facilitators, regional planning, historic preservation, conservation easements, development rights, sustainable farming, comprehensive planning, growth management, consensus.

Who is behind it?

ICLEI – Local Governments for Sustainability (formally, International Council for Local Environmental Initiatives). Communities pay ICLEI dues to provide "local" community plans, software, training, etc. Additional groups include American Planning Council, The Renaissance Planning Group, International City/ County Management Group, aided by US Mayors Conference, National Governors Association, National League of Cities, National Association of County Administrators and many more private organizations and official government agencies. Foundation and government grants drive the process.

Where did it originate?

The term Sustainable Development was first introduced to the world in the pages of a 1987 report (Our Common Future) produced by the United Nations World Commission on Environmental and Development, authored by Gro Harlem Brundtland, VP of the World

Socialist Party. The term was first offered as official UN policy in 1992, in a document called UN Sustainable Development Agenda 21, issued at the UN's Earth Summit, today referred to simply as Agenda 21.

What gives Agenda 21 Ruling Authority?

More than 178 nations adopted Agenda 21 as official policy during a signing ceremony at the Earth Summit. US president George H.W. Bush signed the document for the US. In signing, each nation pledged to adopt the goals of Agenda 21. In 1995, President Bill Clinton, in compliance with Agenda 21, signed Executive Order #12858 to create the President's Council on Sustainable Development in order to "harmonize" US environmental policy with UN directives as outlined in Agenda 21. The EO directed all agencies of the Federal Government to work with state and local community governments in a joint effort "reinvent" government using the guidelines outlined in Agenda 21. As a result, with the assistance of groups like ICLEI, Sustainable Development is now emerging as government policy in every town, county and state in the nation.

Revealing Quotes From the Planners

"Agenda 21 proposes an array of actions which are intended to be implemented by EVERY person on Earth...it calls for specific changes in the activities of ALL people... Effective execution of Agenda 21 will REQUIRE a profound reorientation of ALL humans, unlike anything the world has ever experienced... " Agenda 21: The Earth Summit Strategy to Save Our Planet (Earthpress, 1993).

Urgent to implement – but we don't know what it is!

"The realities of life on our planet dictate that continued economic development as we know it cannot be sustained...Sustainable development, therefore is a program of action for local and global economic reform – a program that has yet to be fully defined." The Local Agenda 21 Planning Guide, published by ICLEI, 1996.

"No one fully understands how or even, if, sustainable development can be achieved; however, there is growing consensus that it must be accomplished at the local level if it is ever to be achieved on a global basis." The Local Agenda 21 Planning Guide, published by ICLEI, 1996.

Agenda 21 and Private Property

"Land...cannot be treated as an ordinary asset, controlled by individuals and subject to the pressures and inefficiencies of the market. Private land ownership is also a principle instrument of accumulation and concentration of wealth, therefore contributes to social injustice." From the report from the 1976 UN's Habitat I Conference.

"Private land use decisions are often driven by strong economic incentives that result in several ecological and aesthetic consequences...The key to overcoming it is through public policy..." Report from the President's Council on Sustainable Development, page 112.

"Current lifestyles and consumption patterns of the affluent middle class – involving high meat intake, use of fossil fuels, appliances, home and work air conditioning, and suburban housing are not sustainable." Maurice Strong, Secretary General of the UN's Earth Summit, 1992.

Reinvention of Government

"We need a new collaborative decision process that leads to better decisions, more rapid change, and more sensible use of human, natural and financial resources in achieving our goals." Report from the President's Council on Sustainable Development.

"Individual rights will have to take a back seat to the collective." Harvey Ruvin, Vice Chairman, ICLEI. The Wildlands Project.

"We must make this place an insecure and inhospitable place for Capitalists and their projects – we must reclaim the roads and plowed lands, halt dam construction, tear down existing dams, free shackled rivers and return to wilderness millions of tens of millions of acres or presently settled land." Dave Foreman, Earth First.

What is not sustainable?

Ski runs, grazing of livestock, plowing of soil, building fences, industry, single family homes, paves and tarred roads, logging activities, dams and reservoirs, power line construction, and economic systems that fail to set proper value on the environment." UN's Biodiversity Assessment Report.

Hide Agenda 21's UN roots from the people

"Participating in a UN advocated planning process would very likely bring out many of the conspiracy- fixated groups and individuals in our society... This segment of our society who fear 'one-world government' and a UN invasion of the United States through which our individual freedom would be stripped away would actively work to defeat any elected official who joined 'the conspiracy' by undertaking LA21. So we call our process something else, such as comprehensive planning, growth management or smart growth." J. Gary Lawrence, advisor to President Clinton's Council on Sustainable Development." End of article.

An article from therightscoop.com advertises a video by John Anthony that, according to the article, explains Agenda 21 more fully. Therightscoop.com article is an advertisement but it also exposes interesting questions about Agenda 21. It states:

"Sustainable developers have designed a global movement coordinated through a global-to-local action plan to create world government in accordance with certain objectives. These objectives include:

1. An end to national sovereignty
2. Abolition of private property
3. Restructure of the family unit
4. Increasing limitations and restrictions on mobility and individual opportunity.

This is a plan that's been underway since the 80s and three presidents have signed off on it, starting with George H. W. Bush. It's already at the local level in the U.S. – even my city has a sustainability council.

Agenda 21 Course: If you are reading this, you must want to know more about Agenda 21. Well, good news-you have arrived at the right place!

This is the site of possibly the only Agenda 21 Course on the Internet. When you are done with the ten topical lessons and the accompanying materials, you will understand what Agenda 21 is and its full impact on you, your family, and your country. Further, you will have enough knowledge to go out into your community and begin to change the course of America-for the better! Do not hesitate. Dive right into Lesson 1-Introduction to Agenda 21.

Lesson 1:Learn the definition, short history, and the 3 E's of Agenda 21.

Lesson 2: How America has been made to accept the scam called Agenda 21.

Lesson 3: How through the Wildlands Project private property rights will be destroyed and a One World Order implemented.

Lesson 4: Once confined to human settlements human behavior must be strictly controlled by Smart Growth strategies.

Lesson 5: Taking control of Wall Street and Main Street and their associated wealth must occur to create a One World Order.

Lesson 6: How the Feds use grants to help implement Agenda 21.

Lesson 7: Regional governments, created by the fed. gov't., use grants funneled down from the fed. gov't. to undermine the control of our local representative government.

Lesson 8: Explains how our people must be dummied down and indoctrinated to create good Global Citizens who think that they are here to serve the needs of the government (includes info. on Common Core).

Lesson 9: Explains how Non Governmental Organizations (such as the Sierra Club, Zero Population Growth, etc.) use of the Delphi Method to implement Agenda 21.

Lesson 10: Many ideas for how to activate yourself to stop the implementation of Agenda 21." End of article.

What does this all mean? Perhaps the One World Order (New World Order) is the goal of our international and national leaders; perhaps Agenda 21 is their strategy to form and implement the One World Order; perhaps the insidious individual parts are the tactics they are using to strip us of our human rights and our opportunity to seek and find individual fulfillment and happiness. The concept of 'social justice' mentioned above must also be considered. It's part of this grand scheme for some powerful people to control the world - and every individual in the world. It must be exposed.

This is another article from wordpress.com, 10-20-2009, that stresses the importance of understanding the devious scheme of Agenda 21. It first references one of the U.N.'s source documents:

"THE ROBINHOOD PLAN aka Agenda 21

(Agenda21 http://www.un.org/esa/dsd/agenda21/)

Let me make this easy for you. The UN has devised a plan where upon they take from the rich (you and I and anyone else in the world that works for a living) and give to the poor (those countries who refuse to elevate themselves due to corrupt governments, societal concerns, etc..) Just like "Oil for Food" however, the real plan is just to steal our money and institute a mafia like system to bully us into cooperation. Here are a small sampling of documents, aka Policy Briefs, put out in preparation of the Copenhagen meeting. It is definitely worth the small investment of time for you to browse them.

There is only one conclusion I reach. If our president signs this he has committed treason. By all accounts he will sign and his friends in the Senate will ratify. They have already started to funnel your money to the IMF and World Bank. I have reported in previous columns the billions of dollars just within the past year which have been given to these institutions through the "Stimulus" Plan and other "Crisis" legislation. The only thing that's being stimulated in this country is the blood pressure of all those who are paying attention.

Saturday, October 24th is the anniversary of the UN. I will be attending a protest in my own small home town. If there is not one scheduled in your town, call your fellow patriots into action. We need to let them know we get it and we will not allow them to sign our futures away in December. Call your Senators and Representatives and tell them you know. Tell them NO WAY! It's beginning to be a daily ritual in my household – perhaps it should be in yours as well.

You may think they aren't listening, but sources tell us they hear, even if they aren't acknowledging it publicly. They don't acknowledge so as to dissuade us from "annoying" them any further. As the old saying goes – change must start with you.

As discussed over the weekend in the column linked above, the consensus is international treaties supersede our constitution. From what I have been told, the only way to get out of a treaty is if the parties involve excuse you. Agenda 21 is structured to punish the US for their success. We will bare the burden. They will not excuse us – we're the goose who lays the golden eggs. President Obama must not be allowed to sign this treaty. Make it clear NOW. Saturday is your opportunity to stand up and be heard. If you do organize a gathering in your town, make sure to let the media and your Senators and Representatives know about it. Take photos, take movies and post them to the internet."

Wordpress.com gives more information explaining the Agenda 21 and the Maurice Strong interconnection:

" According to financial experts, the world as we know it, will change dramatically by the year 2012. People, who provided for their families only three years ago, will be desperately searching for food. The story of the economic meltdown of 2008 begins and ends with the United Nations and its carefully managed One World Order. Behind the curtain of this dark chapter in human misery are ogres Maurice Strong and George Soros.

It is both power lust and an all-consuming hatred of the United States of America that elevated this deadly duo to ogre status. Fortunately for all of those searching for answers, much of their plan for the world, post November 4, 2008 is already mapped out in writing. Leading economic experts and Strong agree that in 2012 people will be going hungry.

"Strong has worked diligently and effectively to bring his ideas to fruition, He is now in a position to implement them." (Henry Lamb, The Rise of Global Governance, available at soverignty.net). "His speeches and writings provide a clear picture of what to expect. In 1991, Strong wrote the introduction to a book published by the Trilateral Commission, called Beyond Interdependence: The Meshing of the World's Economy and the Earth's Ecology, by Jim MacNeil. (David Rockefeller wrote the foreword). Strong said this:

"This interlocking…is the new reality of the century, with profound implications for the shape of our institutions of governance, national and international. By the year 2012, these changes must be fully integrated into our economic and political life."

These chilling words are in line with ones he used for the opening session of the Rio Conference (Earth Summit II) in 1992, that industrialized countries have:

"Developed and benefitted from the unsustainable patterns of production and consumption which have produced our present dilemma. It is clear that current lifestyles and consumption patterns of the affluent middle class—involving high meat intake, consumption of large amounts of frozen and convenience foods, use of fossil fuels, appliances, home and work-place air-conditioning, and suburban housing—are not sustainable. A shift is necessary toward lifestyles less geared to environmentally damaging consumption patterns."

The only change that has happened since 1992 is that Strong and Soros now have their Agent of Change coming to the White House.

Voluntary acceptance of global governance is the preferred means of achieving a takeover of America without a single shot being fired." End of article.

If and when Agenda 21 if fully implemented, will it be possible for a one-world government, or a one-world leader to control every single individual on this planet? Absolutely! The plans are already being made; it's in the form of the new NSA center in Bluffdale, Utah. When completed, that computer will have the capacity to know everything about every individual on earth (all six or seven billion,) including all emails and phone calls, for twenty years. This event has also been clearly prophesied in the Bible - over 2000 years ago in the Book of Revelation: Chapter 13, Verses 15-18.

15, And he had power to give life unto the image of the beast, (that great controlling computer) that the image of the beast should both speak, and cause that as many as would not worship the image of the beast should be killed.

16, And he causeth all, both small and great, rich and poor, free and bond, to receive a mark in their right hand, or in their foreheads:

17, And that no man might buy or sell, save he that had the mark, or the name of the beast, or the number of his name.

18, Here is wisdom. Let him that hath understanding count the number of the beast: for it is the number of a man; and his number is Six hundred threescore and six (666.)

This last verse, 18, says to count the number of a man; and his number is 666. The only way to count that number is to add 6+6+6. That gives the number 18. Perhaps the man's name will have a total of 18 letters. The verse doesn't say interpret the number. It says to 'count' the number. What is the secret password to gain this number by adding? The secret password is that it's presented in **Verse 18**.

— — — — — - — — — — — — — - — — — — —

Social justice in general, and as included in Agenda 21, will be discussed next.

Chapter 3

Social Justice

This is an article submitted by Barry Loberfeld. It was published by FrontPageMagazine.com on February 27, 2004. The title of the article is: 'Social Justice: Code for Communism.'

The signature of modern leftist rhetoric is the deployment of terminology that simply cannot fail to command assent. As Orwell himself recognized, even slavery could be sold if labeled "freedom." In this vein, who could ever conscientiously oppose the pursuit of "social justice," -- i.e., a just society?

To understand "social justice," we must contrast it with the earlier view of justice against which it was conceived -- one that arose as a revolt against political absolutism. With a government (e.g., a monarchy) that is granted absolute power, it is impossible to speak of any injustice on its part. If it can do anything, it can't do anything "wrong." Justice as a political/legal term can begin only when limitations are placed upon the sovereign, i.e., when men define what is unjust for government to do. The historical realization traces from the Roman senate to Magna Carta to the U.S. Constitution to the 19th century. It was now a matter of "justice" that government not arrest citizens arbitrarily, sanction their bondage by others, persecute them for their religion or speech, seize their property, or prevent their travel.

This culmination of centuries of ideas and struggles became known as liberalism. And it was precisely in opposition to this liberalism -- not feudalism or theocracy or the ancien régime, much less 20th century fascism -- that Karl Marx formed and detailed the popular concept of "social justice," (which has become a kind of "new and improved" substitute for a storeful of other terms -- Marxism, socialism, collectivism -- that, in the wake of Communism's history and collapse, are now unsellable).

"The history of all existing society," he and Engels declared, "is the history of class struggles. Freeman and slave, patrician and plebian, lord and serf ... oppressor and oppressed, stood in sharp opposition to each other." They were quite right to note the political castes and resulting clashes of the pre-liberal era. The expositors of liberalism (Spencer, Maine) saw their ethic, by establishing the political equality of all (e.g., the abolition of slavery, serfdom, and inequality of rights), as moving mankind from a "society of status" to a "society of contract." Alas, Marx the Prophet could not accept that the classless millennium had arrived before he did. Thus, he revealed to a benighted humanity that liberalism was in fact merely another stage of History's class struggle -- "capitalism" -- with its own combatants: the "proletariat" and the "bourgeoisie." The former were manual laborers, the latter professionals and business owners. Marx's "classes" were not political castes but occupations.

Today the terms have broadened to mean essentially income brackets. If Smith can make a nice living from his writing, he's a bourgeois; if Jones is reciting poetry for coins in a subway terminal, he's a proletarian. But the freedoms of speech and enterprise that they share equally are "nothing but lies and falsehoods so long as" their differences in affluence and influence persist (Luxemburg). The unbroken line from The Communist Manifesto to its contemporary adherents is that economic inequality is the monstrous injustice of the capitalist system, which must be replaced by an ideal of "social justice" -- a "classless" society created by the elimination of all differences in wealth and "power."

Give Marx his due: He was absolutely correct in identifying the political freedom of liberalism -- the right of each man to do as he wishes with his own resources -- as the origin of income disparity under capitalism. If Smith is now earning a fortune while Jones is still stuck in that subway, it's not because of the "class" into which each was born, to say nothing of royal patronage. They are where they are because of how the common man spends his money. That's why some writers sell books in the millions, some sell them in the thousands, and still others can't even get published. It is the choices of the masses ("the market") that create the inequalities of fortune and fame -- and the only way to correct those "injustices" is to control those choices.

Every policy item on the leftist agenda is merely a deduction from this fundamental premise. Private property and the free market of exchange are the most obvious hindrances to the implementation of that agenda, but hardly the only. Also verboten is the choice to emigrate, which removes one and one's wealth from the pool of resources to be redirected by the demands of "social justice" and its enforcers. And crucial to the justification of a "classless" society is the undermining of any notion that individuals are responsible for their behavior and its consequences. To maintain the illusion that classes still exist under capitalism, it cannot be conceded that the "haves" are responsible for what they have or that the "have nots" are responsible for what they have not. Therefore, people are what they are because of where they were born into the social order -- as if this were early 17th century France.

Men of achievement are pointedly referred to as "the privileged" -- as if they were given everything and earned nothing. Their seeming accomplishments are, at best, really nothing more than the results of the sheer luck of a beneficial social environment (or even -- in the allowance of one egalitarian, John Rawls -- "natural endowment"). Consequently, the "haves" do not deserve what they have. The flip side of this is the insistence that the "have nots" are, in fact, "the underprivileged," who have been denied their due by an unjust society. If some men wind up behind bars, they are (to borrow from Broadway) depraved only because they are "deprived." Environmental determinism, once an almost sacred doctrine of official Soviet academe, thrives as the "social constructionist" orthodoxy of today's anti-capitalist left. The theory of "behavioral scientists" and their boxed rats serviceably parallels the practice of a Central Planning Board and its closed society.

The imperative of economic equality also generates a striking opposition between "social justice" and its liberal rival. The equality of the latter, we've noted, is the equality of all individuals in the eyes of the law -- the protection of the political rights of each man, irrespective of "class" (or any assigned collective identity, hence the blindfold of Justice personified). However, this political equality, also noted, spawns the difference in "class" between Smith and Jones. All this echoes Nobel laureate F.A. Hayek's observation that if "we treat them equally [politically], the result must be inequality in their actual [i.e., economic] position." The irresistible conclusion is that "the only way to place them in an equal [economic] position would be to treat them differently [politically]" -- precisely the conclusion that the advocates of "social justice" themselves have always reached.

In the nations that had instituted this resolution throughout their legal systems, "different" political treatment came to subsume the extermination or imprisonment of millions because of their "class" origins. In our own American "mixed economy," which mixes differing systems of justice as much as economics, "social justice" finds expression in such policies and propositions as progressive taxation and income redistribution; affirmative action and even "reparations," its logical implication; and selective censorship in the name of "substantive equality," i.e., economic equality disingenuously reconfigured as a Fourteenth Amendment right and touted as the moral superior to "formal equality," the equality of political freedom actually guaranteed by the amendment.

This last is the project of a growing number of leftist legal theorists that includes Cass Sunstein and Catherine MacKinnon, the latter opining that the "law of [substantive] equality and the law of freedom of expression [for all] are on a collision course in this country." Interestingly, Hayek had continued, "Equality before the law and material equality are, therefore, not only different, but in conflict with each other" -- a pronouncement that evidently draws no dissent.

Hayek emphasized another conflict between the two conceptions of justice, one we can begin examining simply by asking who the subject of liberal justice is. The answer: a person -- a flesh-and-blood person, who is held accountable for only those actions that constitute specifically defined crimes of violence (robbery, rape, murder) against other citizens. Conversely, who is the subject of "social justice" -- society? Indeed yes, but is society really a "who"?

When we speak of "social psychology" (the standard example), no one believes that there is a "social psyche" whose thoughts can be analyzed. And yet the very notion of "social justice" presupposes a volitional Society whose actions can (and must) be held accountable. This jarring bit of Platonism traces all the way back to Marx himself, who, "despite all his anti-Idealistic and anti-Hegelian rhetoric, is really an Idealist and Hegelian ... asserting, at root, that [Society] precedes and determines the characteristics of those who are [its] members" (R.A. Childs, Jr.). Behold leftism's alternative to liberalism's "atomistic individualism": reifying collectivism, what Hayek called "anthropomorphism or personification."

Too obviously, it is not liberalism that atomizes an entity (a concrete), but "social justice" that reifies an aggregate (an abstraction). And exactly what injustice is Society responsible for? Of course: the economic inequality between Smith and Jones -- and Johnson and Brown and all others. But there is no personified Society who planned and perpetrated this alleged inequity, only a society of persons acting upon the many choices made by their individual minds. Eventually, though, everyone recognizes that this Ideal of Society doesn't exist in the real world -- leaving two options. One is to cease holding society accountable as a legal entity, a moral agent. The other is to conclude that the only practicable way to hold society accountable for "its" actions is to police the every action of every individual.

The apologists for applied "social justice" have always explained away its relationship to totalitarianism as nothing more than what we may call (after Orwell's Animal Farm) the "Napoleon scenario": the subversion of earnest revolutions by demented individuals (e.g., Stalin, Mao -- to name just two among too many). What can never be admitted is that authoritarian brutality is the not-merely-possible-but-inevitable realization of the nature of "social justice" itself.

What is "social justice"? The theory that implies and justifies the practice of socialism. And what is "socialism"? Domination by the State. What is "socialized" is state-controlled. So what is "totalitarian" socialism other than total socialism, i.e., state control of everything? And what is that but the absence of a free market in anything, be it goods or ideas? Those who contend that a socialist government need not be totalitarian, that it can allow a free market -- independent choice, the very source of "inequality"! -- in some things (ideas) and not in others (goods -- as if, say, books were one or the other), are saying only that the socialist ethic shouldn't be applied consistently.

This is nothing less than a confession of moral cowardice. It is the explanation for why, from Moscow to Managua, all the rivalries within the different socialist revolutions have been won by, not the "democratic" or "libertarian" socialists, but the totalitarians, i.e., those who don't qualify their socialism with antonyms. "Totalitarian socialism" is not a variation but a redundancy, which is why half-capitalist hypocrites will always lose out to those who have the courage of their socialist convictions. (Likewise, someone whose idea of "social justice" is a moderate welfare state is someone who's willing to tolerate far more "social injustice" than he's willing to eliminate.)

What is "social justice"? The abolition of privacy. Its repudiation of property rights, far from being a fundamental, is merely one derivation of this basic principle. Socialism, declared Marx, advocates "the positive abolition of private property [in order to effect] the return of man himself as a social, i.e., really human, being." It is the private status of property -- meaning: the privacy, not the property -- that stands in opposition to the social (i.e., "socialized," and thus "really human") nature of man. Observe that the premise holds even when we substitute x for property. If private anything denies man's social nature, then so does private everything. And it is the negation of anything and everything private -- from work to worship to even family life -- that has been the social affirmation of the socialist state.

What is "social justice"? The opposite of capitalism. And what is "capitalism"? It is Marx's coinage (minted by his materialist dispensation) for the Western liberalism that diminished state power from absolutism to limited government; that, from John Locke to the American Founders, held that each individual has an inviolable right to his own life, liberty, and property, which government exists solely to secure. Now what would the reverse of this be but a resurrection of Oriental despotism, the reactionary increase of state power from limited government to absolutism, i.e., "totalitarianism," the absolute control of absolutely everything? And what is the opposite -- the violation -- of securing the life, liberty, and property of all men other than mass murder, mass tyranny, and mass plunder? And what is that but the point at which theory ends and history begins?

And yet even before that point -- before the 20th century, before publication of the Manifesto itself -- there were those who did indeed make the connection between what Marxism inherently meant on paper and what it would inevitably mean in practice. In 1844, Arnold Ruge presented the abstract: "a police and slave state." And in 1872, Michael Bakunin provided the specifics:

"The People's State of Marx ... will not content itself with administering and governing the masses politically, as all governments do today. It will also administer the masses economically, concentrating in the hands of the State the production and division of wealth, the cultivation of land, the establishment and development of factories, the organization and direction of commerce, and finally the application of capital to production by the only banker -- the State. All that will demand an immense knowledge and many heads "overflowing with brains" in this government. It will be the reign of scientific intelligence, the most aristocratic, despotic, arrogant, and elitist of all regimes. There will be a new class, a new hierarchy of real and counterfeit scientists and scholars, and the world will be divided into a minority ruling in the name of knowledge, and an immense ignorant majority. And then, woe unto the mass of ignorant ones!"

It is precisely this "new class" that reflects the defining contradiction of modern leftist reality: The goal of complete economic equality logically enjoins the means of complete state control, yet this means has never practically achieved that end. Yes, Smith and Jones, once "socialized," are equally poor and equally oppressed, but now above them looms an oligarchy of not-to-be-equalized equalizers. The inescapable rise of this "new class" -- privileged economically as well as politically, never quite ready to "wither away" -- forever destroys the possibility of a "classless" society. Here the lesson of socialism teaches what should have been learned from the lesson of pre-liberal despotism -- that state coercion is a means to no end but its own. Far from expanding equality from the political to the economic realm, the pursuit of "social justice" serves only to contract it within both. There will never be any kind of equality -- or real justice -- as long as a socialist elite stands behind the trigger while the rest of us kneel before the barrel.

The contemporary left remains possessed by the spirit of Marx, present even where he's not, and the best overview of his ideology remains Thomas Sowell's Marxism: Philosophy and Economics, which is complemented perfectly by the most accessible refutation of that ideology, David Conway's A Farewell to Marx. Hayek's majestic The Mirage of Social Justice is a challenging yet rewarding effort, while his The Road to Serfdom provides an unparalleled exposition of how freedom falls to tyranny. Moving from theory to practice, Communism: A History, Richard Pipes' slim survey, ably says all that is needed. End of article by Barry Loberfeld.

This quote is from an article by William Sullivan on Theamericanthinker.com, 10-2012, titled: 'Social Justice is a Proven Failure - So is Obama.'

"Obama's vision for America is based upon equality, not liberty. And despite the apparent confusion that many Americans seem to have, these two principles do not represent the same thing. But don't take my word for it. Milton Friedman, the brilliant economist and advisor to Ronald Reagan, has clarified the distinction between equality and liberty in the clearest of terms, and it doesn't take a political mind to grasp it. It just takes a mind willing to accept reality.

While fielding questions before an audience at Stanford University on February 9th, 1978, Friedman was challenged by a young man in the audience about America's responsibility to the poor.

The young man began:

"You say that many people in America agree with your kind of freedom, a freedom from coercion, and I might agree with you. But I also believe that many people in America believe in a different kind of freedom, and that is freedom to well-being. A certain level of standards for housing at a good price, education, et cetera. Also, I want to say that the state has built into it a system, uh, ah, that the poor remain poor and the rich remain rich. And that is an externality of the system."

Another way of putting this is to say that he believes that income inequality is a serious problem that is only getting worse because of systemic flaws that cause the rich to get richer and the poor to get poorer, which is precisely how Obama frames the issue. So Friedman's response to this suggestion applies equally:

"It is not built into the system at all. It has never been true. It is simply false. If you look at the evidence, there's an enormous amount of mobility from one class to the other. In fact there used to be a saying "Three generations from shirtsleeves to shirtsleeves," which reflected exactly the opposite effect. It is not built into the system. On the contrary, there is a great deal of mobility within generations and between generations. So we shouldn't argue on the basis of false factual premises."

Oh, if only we didn't have to argue on the basis of false premises, we could be free of this myth once and for all. The plain and simple fact is that the vast majority of Americans generally do not remain in either the "poor" income class or the "rich." As Friedman's contemporary Thomas Sowell points out, "Comparing the top income bracket to the bottom income bracket for a period of years tells you nothing about what is happening to the actual flesh and blood human beings who are moving between brackets during those years."

Fluidity between income classes is not only possible but distinctly likely for most Americans, who at one time or another file taxes as singles while making minimum wage, and are therefore considered "poor." Later in life, of course, those same Americans increase their skill set and marketability to the point that they can earn more money, and thus, they are no longer "poor."

This is an interesting prospect, isn't it? At one point in your life, you were probably a number that contributed to a statistic that a leftist social engineer pointed to as evidence of "economic inequality." Many Americans have moved beyond their role as evidence of "poverty," but other young, unskilled earners have taken their place, and thus, poverty is still the epidemic that it was when you shared the burden of this systematically applied "poverty."

Data, ascertained and interpreted in this manner, becomes political fodder, not a reflection of facts, and not reflective of American society.

Nonetheless, the young man was unmoved by Friedman's explanation, and suggested:

"Because it is not immediately easy to become in the wealthy class, there are certain parts of the system that make that virtually impossible for the real person."

This exposes a magnificent fallacy. There is a wide chasm between incredible success and incredible failure. We Americans call it the "middle class," to which most of us belong. It seems silly, but it's necessary to note that moderate success and moderate failure exist in that broad area between. Here, this young man is arguing for the state's responsibility to create "ladders of opportunity" out of poverty. Again, this is a position that our president has taken on many occasions. The young man went on, and surprisingly, with a very substantial question:

"I believe that this freedom, too, represents the freedom to equality, as opposed to liberty. And I wonder, is it possible to build a system based on this equality that I think most people agree in, and would not be willing to sacrifice to the liberty of freedom from?"

After a disclosure that his response was a simple matter of "thought" and "reason," Friedman offered the profound response:

"In my opinion, a society that aims for equality before liberty, will end up with neither equality nor liberty. And a society that aims first for liberty, will not end up with equality, but with it will end up with a closer approach to equality than any other kind of system that has ever been developed. Now that conclusion is based both on evidence from history -- across history -- and also, I believe, on reasoning, which, if you try to follow through the implications of aiming first at equality, will become clear to you. You can only aim at equality, by giving some people the right to take things from others. And what ultimately happens when you aim at equality is that A and B decide what C shall do for D. Except that they take a little bit of a commission off on the way."

That kind of says it all. The truth is that Barack Obama's vision for America entails a scenario where he can provide his promised equality, or "social justice," by giving a select few people in Washington the right to "take things from others." Nothing about that amounts to liberty; it's all about establishing equality. It is a vision that has been exposed for decades as a simplistic idea that cannot attain reality without the aid of tyranny. It has been tried many times in history. And it has failed in every application, just as it has obviously failed during Obama's tenure as president.

We cannot afford Americans being ignorant of this reality any longer." End of article.

Social Justice is also the major foundation for Saul Alinsky's concept of 'Rules for Radicals.' These rules seem the basis of much argument from those who propose government become more intrusive and controlling of individuals' daily life.

I got this information in an email, but forgot the origin. The sender asked recipients to 'pass it on.' It concerns the influence of Saul Alinsky on our current politics. It also helps explain why there is such deep division between the ideology of governing between 'liberals' and 'conservatives.':

"Saul Alinsky died about 43 years ago, but his writings continue to influence many in political control of our nation today. Hillary Clinton did her college thesis on his writings and Obama writes about him in his books.

Alinsky's important books are: 'Rules for Radicals' and 'Reveille for Radicals.' In the books he explains how to create a social state. According to him there are eight levels of control that must be obtained before you are able to create a social state. The first is the most important:

1) Healthcare– Control healthcare and you control the people.

2) Poverty – Increase the poverty level as high as possible, poor people are easier to control and will not fight back if you are providing everything for them to live.

3) Debt – Increase the debt to an unsustainable level. That way you are able to increase taxes, and this will produce more poverty.

4) Gun Control– Remove the ability to defend themselves from the government. That way you are able to create a police state.

5) Welfare – Take control of every aspect of their lives (Food, Housing, and Income.)

6) Education – Take control of what people read and listen to – take control of what children learn in school.

7) Religion – Remove the belief in the God from the Government and schools.

8) Class Warfare – Divide the people into the wealthy and the poor. This will cause more discontent and it will be easier to take (Tax) the wealthy with the support of the poor."

Alinsky merely simplified Vladimir Lenin's original scheme for world conquest by communism, under Russian rule. Stalin described his converts as "Useful Idiots." The Useful Idiots have destroyed every nation in which they have seized power and control. It is presently happening at an alarming rate in the U.S. According to Alinsky: "It is difficult to free fools from the chains they revere."

I had never heard that term before, "Useful Idiots," so I went to Wikipedia. This is part of the Wikipedia description:

"In political jargon, useful idiot is a term for people perceived as propagandists for a cause whose goals they are not fully aware of, and who are used cynically by the leaders of the cause.

Despite often being attributed to Lenin, in 1987, Grant Harris, senior reference librarian at the Library of Congress, declared that "We have not been able to identify this phrase among [Lenin's] published works."

In Russian language, the equivalent term "useful fools" was in use at least in 1941.

A similar term, useful innocents, appears in Austrian-American economist Ludwig von Mises's "Planned Chaos" (1947). Von Mises claims the term was used by communists for liberals that von Mises describes as "confused and misguided sympathizers". The term useful innocents also appears in a Readers Digest article (1946) titled "Yugoslavia's Tragic Lesson to the World", an excerpt from a, at the time, forthcoming book (no title printed) authored by Bogdan Raditsa (Bogdan Radica), a "high ranking official of the Yugoslav Government". Raditsa says: "In the Serbo-Croat language the communists have a phrase for true democrats who consent to collaborate with them for 'democracy.' It is Korisne Budale, or Useful Innocents." Although Raditsa translates the phrase as "Useful Innocents", the word budala (plural: budale) actually translates as "fool" and synonyms thereof."

This is another article, posted by Meredith Jessup, August 14, 2012, which explains more about the connection between Agenda 21 and social justice. It's titled, 'How Obama is using policy to pursue social justice:'

"Forbes has an interesting article posted today by Stanley Kurtz who writes about how Obama's policies rob the suburbs to pay for the cities:

Political experts left and right agree: the coming election will be decided by America's suburbanites. From Florida to Virginia on across the country, in every battleground state, they are the key demographic. All of which raises a question that has not been considered as yet, and ought to be: is President Obama's re-election in the suburbanites' interest? The answer emphatically is no.

As many Americans do not know, in the eyes of the leftist community organizers who trained Obama, suburbs are instruments of bigotry and greed — a way of selfishly refusing to share tax money with the urban poor. Obama adopted this view early on, and he has never wavered from this ideological commitment, as a review of his actions in office goes to show.

President Obama's plans for a second-term include an initiative to systematically redistribute the wealth of America's suburbs to the cities. It's a transformative idea, and deserves to be fully aired before the election. But like a lot of his major progressive policy innovations, Obama has advanced this one stealthily—mostly through rule-making, appointment, and vague directives. Obama has worked on this project in collaboration with Mike Kruglik, one of his original community organizing mentors. Kruglik's new group, Building One America, advocates "regional tax-base sharing," a practice by which suburban tax money is directly redistributed to nearby cities and less-well-off "inner-ring" suburbs. Kruglik's group also favors a raft of policies designed to coerce people out of their cars and force suburbanites (with their tax money) back into densely packed cities.

Obama has lent the full weight of his White House to Kruglik's efforts. A federal program called the Sustainable Communities Initiative, for example, has salted planning commissions across the country with "regional equity" and "smart growth" as goals. These are, of course, code words. "Regional equity" means that, by their mere existence, suburbs cheat the people who live in cities. It means, "Let's spread the suburbs' wealth around" – i.e., take from the suburbanites to give to the urban poor. "Smart growth" means, "Quit building sub-divisions and malls, and move back to where mass transit can shuttle you between your 800 square foot apartment in an urban tower and your downtown job." In all likelihood, these planning commissions will issue "recommendations" which Obama would quickly turn into requirements for further federal aid. In fact, his administration has already used these tactics to impose federal education requirements on reluctant states. Indeed, part of Obama's assault on the suburbs is his effort to undercut the autonomy of suburban school districts.

I thought this article was especially interesting given my own personal experiences in the state of Michigan. Talk to local government officials here and they all say the same thing — local transportation and housing are where the money is these days.

The federal government is pouring billions into local transportation, agricultural and environmental projects to create "sustainable communities" – to tell Americans where to live and how to travel:

While some may hope this effort is nothing more than the President's attempt to use the White House as a bully pulpit to encourage Americans to mimic the urbane lifestyle he experienced in an upscale Chicago neighborhood, the record of past such efforts by the federal government is more troubling.

In January 1998, President Bill Clinton's Environmental Protection Agency threatened to withhold federal transportation funds from the Atlanta region because it did not meet federal air-quality standards and said that it would agree to restore the funding only if the state of Georgia dramatically altered its land-use and transportation policies in ways similar to those characteristic of the Smart Growth polices that discourage single-family detached housing and encourage public transit use and investment. Georgia agreed to do this, at least through the waning days of the Clinton Administration, but soon abandoned the policies when leadership in Washington changed.

Carol Browner headed the EPA when the threat was imposed on Atlanta under Clinton. Today, she is Assistant to the President for Energy and Climate Change. With the prospect of even worse to come from this new DOT-HUD partnership on sustainable communities, those who are skeptical of the President's grandiose efforts at social engineering should be on the alert.

The sheer amount of money being handed down from the federal government is staggering, according to local officials. So staggering, in fact, they had to get creative in finding ways to use all of it. What did they come up with? In one city close to my home, for example, they've developed a new, state-of-the-art office complex for city transportation workers, complete with multiple flat-screen televisions in every office, a fitness center for employees that never gets used and millions of dollars in phone and video conferencing equipment that no one knows how to operate. In addition, they've spent millions on equipping city buses with GPS monitoring systems so that riders with smartphones can track when their bus will arrive down to the minute — priority stuff, obviously.

But who cares about the cost? When it's not their money, they have no worries in spending it.

Grants that fund these projects come from federal agencies and programs, including the "New Freedom" program.

(I'm sure it's pure coincidence, but "New Freedom" is also the historical designation given to progressive hero Woodrow Wilson's first presidential campaign in 1912. In the campaign, Wilson distanced himself from Theodore Roosevelt's "New Nationalism" and insisted on the importance of free enterprise. Once elected, he abandoned the concept, however, and turned to chief economic advisor Louise Brandeis who focused on dismantling and limiting growing businesses. Wilson's "New Freedom" thus greatly extended the power of the federal government in social and economic affairs and paved the way for programs like FDR's New Deal, LBJ's Great Society and Obama's health care overhaul.)

Today, massive federal spending "trickles down" into programs with names like United We Ride — programs all aimed at artificially expanding cities at the expense of those who don't live there. End of article by (Stanley Kurtz) Meredith Jessup.

The One World Order; is it coming? If and when it does it will certainly be escorted into fulfillment by 'social justice.' This was the theme for those who destroyed the once great nations of Russia and Germany. Along the way, in both cases, their war against Christians and God was one of their major strategies to achieve their evil goals - through 'social justice.'

The Third Jihad will be discussed in the next chapter. It's the third arm of the War on Christians. It's amazing that the plan outlined by the 'Explanatory Memorandum On the General Strategic Goal for the Group In North America' is being implemented in broad daylight, right before our eyes; and we wonder why Christianity is not only being pushed to the sidelines - it's being trampled on and spat on - and our government is fervently supporting it.

Chapter 4

The Third Jihad

By
The Muslim Brotherhood

This is an article from Discoverthenetworks.org. It explains the discovery and contents of a document that outlines the destruction of our American way of life by the Islamic group known as the Muslim Brotherhood. It's the underground and insidious attack that's been taking place since Barack Obama's first inaguration:

In July 2007, seven key leaders of an Islamic charity known as the Holy Land Foundation for Relief and Development (HLF) went on trial for charges that they had: (a) provided "material support and resources" to a foreign terrorist organization (namely Hamas); (b) engaged in money laundering; and (c) breached the International Emergency Economic Powers Act, which prohibits transactions that threaten American national security. Along with the seven named defendants, the U.S. government released a list of approximately 300 "unindicted co-conspirators" and "joint venturers." During the course of the HLF trial, many incriminating documents were entered into evidence. Perhaps the most significant of these was "An Explanatory Memorandum on the General Strategic Goal for the Group in North America," by the Muslim Brotherhood operative Mohamed Akram. Federal investigators found Akram's memo in the home of Ismael Elbarasse, a founder of the Dar Al-Hijrah mosque in Falls Church, Virginia, during a 2004 search. Elbarasse was a member of the Palestine Committee, which the Muslim Brotherhood had created to support Hamas in the United States.

Written sometime in 1987 but not formally published until May 22, 1991, Akram's 18-page document listed the Brotherhood's 29 like-minded "organizations of our friends" that shared the common goal of dismantling American institutions and turning the U.S. into a Muslim nation. These "friends" were identified by Akram and the Brotherhood as groups that could help convince Muslims "that their work in America is a kind of grand Jihad in eliminating and destroying the Western civilization from within and 'sabotaging' its miserable house by their hands ... so that ... God's religion [Islam] is made victorious over all other religions."

Akram was well aware that in the U.S., it would be extremely difficult to promote Islam by means of terror attacks. Thus the "grand jihad" that he and his Brotherhood comrades envisioned was not a violent one involving bombings and shootings, but rather a stealth (or "soft") jihad aiming to impose Islamic law (Sharia) over every region of the earth by incremental, non-confrontational means, such as working to "expand the observant Muslim base"; to "unif[y] and direc[t] Muslims' efforts"; and to "present Islam as a civilization alternative." At its heart, Akram's document details a plan to conquer and Islamize the United States – not as an ultimate objective, but merely as a stepping stone toward the larger goal of one day creating "the global Islamic state."

In line with this objective, Akram and the Brotherhood resolved to "settle" Islam and the Islamic movement within the United States, so that the Muslim religion could be "enabled within the souls, minds and the lives of the people of the country." Akram explained that this could be accomplished "through the establishment of firmly-rooted organizations on whose bases civilization, structure and testimony are built." He urged Muslim leaders to make "a shift from the collision mentality to the absorption mentality," meaning that they should abandon any tactics involving defiance or confrontation, and seek instead to implant into the larger society a host of seemingly benign Islamic groups with ostensibly unobjectionable motives; once those groups had gained a measure of public acceptance, they would be in a position to more effectively promote societal transformation by the old Communist technique of "boring from within."

"The heart and the core" of this strategy, said Akram, was contingent upon these groups' ability to develop "a mastery of the art of 'coalitions.'" That is, by working synergistically they could complement, augment, and amplify one another's efforts. Added Akram: "The big challenge that is ahead of us is how to turn these seeds or 'scattered' elements into comprehensive, stable, 'settled' organizations that are connected with our Movement and which fly in our orbit and take orders from our guidance." The ultimate objective was not only an enlarged Muslim presence, but also implementation of the Brotherhood objectives of transforming pluralistic societies, particularly America, into Islamic states, and sweeping away Western notions of legal equality, freedom of conscience, freedom of religion, and freedom of speech.

Akram and the Brotherhood understood that in order to succeed in this endeavor, they needed to appeal to different strata of the American population in different ways; that whereas some people could be influenced by messages delivered from a religious perspective, others would be more responsive to messages delivered by educators, or bankers, or political figures, or journalists, etc. Thus, Akram's blueprint for the advancement of the Islamic movement stressed the need to form a coalition of groups coming from the worlds of education; religious proselytization; political activism; audio and video production; print media; banking and finance; the physical sciences; the social sciences; professional and business networking; cultural affairs; the publishing and distribution of books;

children and teenagers; women's rights; vocational concerns; and jurisprudence.

By promoting the Islamic movement on such a wide variety of fronts, the Brotherhood and its allies could multiply exponentially their influence. Toward that end, the Akram/Brotherhood "Explanatory Memorandum" named 29 groups as the organizations they believed could collaborate effectively to destroy America from within – "if they all march according to one plan."

The memorandum begins:

"In the name of God, the Beneficent, the Merciful Thanks be to God, Lord of the Two Worlds, Prayers and peace be upon the master of the Messengers."

An Explanatory Memorandum
On the General Strategic Goal for the Group In North America 5/22/1991

Contents:

1- An introduction in explanation
2- The Concept of Settlement
3- The Process of Settlement
4- Comprehensive Settlement Organizations

In the name of God,
the Beneficent, the
Merciful Thanks be
to God, Lord of the
Two Worlds And
Blessed are the
Pious

The beloved brother/The General Masul, may God keep him
The beloved brother/Secretary of the Shura Council, may God keep him
The beloved brothers/Members of the Shura Council, may God keep them

God's peace, mercy and blessings be upon you.....to proceed.

I ask Almighty God that you, your families and those whom you love around you are in the best of conditions, pleasing to God, glorified His name be.

I send this letter of mine to you hoping that it would seize your attention and receive your good care as you are the people of responsibility and those to whom trust is given. Between your hands is an "Explanatory Memorandum" which I put effort in writing down so that it is not locked in the chest and the mind, and so that I can share with you a portion of the responsibility in leading the Group in this country.

What might have encouraged me to submit the memorandum in this time in particular is my feeling of a "glimpse of hope" and the beginning of good tidings which bring the good news that we have embarked on a new stage of Islamic activism stages in this continent. The papers which are between your hands are not abundant extravagance, imaginations or hallucinations which passed in the mind of one of your brothers, but they are rather hopes, ambitions and challenges that I hope that you share some or most of which with me. I do not claim their infallibility or absolute correctness, but they are an attempt which requires study, outlook, detailing and rooting from you.

My request to my brothers is to read the memorandum and to write what they wanted of comments and corrections, keeping in mind that what is between your hands is not strange or a new submission without a root, but rather an attempt to interpret and explain some of what came in the long-term plan which we approved and adopted in our council and our conference in the year (1987).

So, my honorable brother, do not rush to throw these papers away due to your many occupations and worries. All what I'm asking of you is to read them and to comment on them hoping that we might continue together the project of our plan and our Islamic work in this part of the world. Should you do that, I would be thankful and grateful to you.

I also ask my honorable brother, the Secretary of the Council, to add the subject of the memorandum on the Council agenda in its coming meeting.

May God reward you good and keep you for His Daw'a
Your brother/Mohamed Akram
In the name of God,
the Beneficent, the
Merciful Thanks be
to God, Lord of the
Two Worlds And
Blessed are the Pious

Subject: A project for an explanatory memorandum for the General

Strategic goal for the Group in North America mentioned in the long-term plan

One: The Memorandum is derived from:

1- The general strategic goal of the Group in America which was approved by the Shura Council and the Organizational Conference for the year [1987] is "Enablement of Islam in North America, meaning: establishing an effective and a stable Islamic Movement led by the Muslim Brotherhood which adopts Muslims' causes domestically and globally, and which works to expand the observant Muslim base, aims at unifying and directing Muslims' efforts, presents Islam as a civilization alternative, and supports the global Islamic State wherever it is".

2- The priority that is approved by the Shura Council for the work of the Group in its current and former session which is "Settlement".

3- The positive development with the brothers in the Islamic Circle in an attempt to reach a unity of merger.

4- The constant need for thinking and future planning, an attempt to read it and working to "shape" the present to comply and suit the needs and challenges of the future.

5- The paper of his eminence, the General Masul, may God keep him, which he recently sent to the members of the Council.

Two: An Introduction to the Explanatory Memorandum:

In order to begin with the explanation, we must "summon" the following question and place it in front of our eyes as its relationship is important and necessary with the strategic goal and the explanation project we are embarking on. The question we are facing is: "How do you like to see the Islam Movement in North America in ten years?", or "taking along" the following sentence when planning and working, "Islamic Work in North America in the year (2000): A Strategic Vision".

Also, we must summon and take along "elements" of the general strategic goal of the Group in North America and I will intentionally repeat them in numbers. They are:

1- Establishing an effective and stable Islamic Movement led by the Muslim Brotherhood.
2- Adopting Muslims' causes domestically and globally.
3- Expanding the observant Muslim base.
4- Unifying and directing Muslims' efforts.
5- Presenting Islam as a civilization alternative
6- Supporting the establishment of the global Islamic State wherever it is.

It must be stressed that it has become clear and emphatically known that all is in agreement that we must "settle" or "enable" Islam and its Movement in this part of the world. Therefore, a joint understanding of the meaning of settlement or enablement must be adopted, through which and on whose basis we explain the general strategic goal with its six elements for the Group in North America.

Three: The Concept of Settlement:

This term was mentioned in the Group's "dictionary" and documents with various meanings in spite of the fact that everyone meant one thing with it. We believe that the understanding of the essence is the same and we will attempt here to give the word and its "meanings" a practical explanation with a practical Movement tone, and not a philosophical linguistic explanation, while stressing that this explanation of ours is not complete until our explanation of "the process" of settlement itself is understood which is mentioned in the following paragraph. We briefly say the following:

Settlement: "That Islam and its Movement become a part of the homeland it lives in". Establishment: "That Islam turns into firmly-rooted organizations on whose bases civilization, structure and testimony are built". Stability: "That Islam is stable in the land on which its people move". Enablement: "That Islam is enabled within the souls, minds and the lives of the people of the country in which it moves". Rooting: "That Islam is resident and not a passing thing, or rooted "entrenched" in the soil of the spot where it moves and not a strange plant to it".

Four : The Process of Settlement:

In order for Islam and its Movement to become "a part of the homeland" in which it lives, "stable" in its land, "rooted" in the spirits and minds of its people, "enabled" in the live of its society and has firmly-established "organizations" on which the Islamic structure is built and with which the testimony of civilization is achieved, the Movement must plan and struggle to obtain "the keys" and the tools of this process in carry out this grand mission as a "Civilization Jihadist" responsibility which lies on the shoulders of Muslims and - on top of them - the Muslim Brotherhood in this country. Among these keys and tools are the following:

1- Adopting the concept of settlement and understanding its practical meanings:
The Explanatory Memorandum focused on the Movement and the realistic dimension of the process of settlement and its practical meanings without

paying attention to the difference in understanding between the resident and the non-resident, or who is the settled and the non-settled and we believe that what was mentioned in the long-term plan in that regards suffices.

2- Making a fundamental shift in our thinking and mentality in order to suit the challenges of the settlement mission.

What is meant with the shift - which is a positive expression - is responding to the grand challenges of the settlement issues. We believe that any transforming response begins with the method of thinking and its center, the brain, first. In order to clarify what is meant with the shift as a key to qualify us to enter the field of settlement, we say very briefly that the following must be accomplished:

A shift from the partial thinking mentality to the comprehensive thinking mentality.

A shift from the "amputated" partial thinking mentality to the "continuous" comprehensive mentality.

A shift from the mentality of caution and reservation to the mentality of risk and controlled liberation.

A shift from the mentality of the elite Movement to the mentality of the popular Movement.

A shift from the mentality of preaching and guidance to the mentality of building and testimony.

A shift from the single opinion mentality to the multiple opinion mentality.

A shift from the collision mentality to the absorption mentality.

A shift from the individual mentality to the team mentality.

A shift from the anticipation mentality to the initiative mentality.

A shift from the hesitation mentality to the decisiveness mentality.

A shift from the principles mentality to the programs mentality.

A shift from the abstract ideas mentality the true organizations mentality [This is the core point and the essence of the memorandum].

3- Understanding the historical stages in which the Islamic Ikhwani activism went through in this country:
The writer of the memorandum believes that understanding and comprehending the historical stages of the Islamic activism which was led and being led by the Muslim Brotherhood in this continent is a very important key in working towards settlement, through which the Group observes its march, the direction of its movement and the curves and turns of its road. We will suffice here with mentioning the title for each of these stages [The title expresses the prevalent characteristic of the stage] [Details maybe mentioned in another future study]. Most likely, the stages are:

A- The stage of searching for self and determining the identity.
B- The stage of inner build-up and tightening the organization.
C- The stage of mosques and the Islamic centers.
D- The stage of building the Islamic organizations - the first phase.
E- The stage of building the Islamic schools - the first phase.
F- The stage of thinking about the overt Islamic Movement - the first phase.
G- The stage of openness to the other Islamic movements and attempting to reach a formula for dealing with them - the first phase.
H- The stage of reviving and establishing the Islamic organizations - the second phase.

We believe that the Group is embarking on this stage in its second phase as it has to open the door and enter as it did the first time.

4-Understanding the role of the Muslim Brother in North America:
The process of settlement is a "Civilization-Jihadist Process" with all the word means. The Ikhwan must understand that their work in America is a

kind of grand Jihad in eliminating and destroying the Western civilization from within and "sabotaging" its miserable house by their hands and the hands of the believers so that it is eliminated and God's religion is made victorious over all other religions. Without this level of understanding, we are not up to this challenge and have not prepared ourselves for Jihad yet. It is a Muslim's destiny to perform Jihad and work wherever he is and wherever he lands until the final hour comes, and there is no escape from that destiny except for those who chose to slack. But, would the slackers and the Mujahedeen be equal.

5-Understanding that we cannot perform the settlement mission by ourselves or away from people:
A mission as significant and as huge as the settlement mission needs magnificent and exhausting efforts. With their capabilities, human, financial and scientific resources, the Ikhwan will not be able to carry out this mission alone or away from people and he who believes that is wrong, and God knows best. As for the role of the Ikhwan, it is the initiative, pioneering, leadership, raising the banner and pushing people in that direction. They are then to work to employ, direct and unify Muslims' efforts and powers for this process. In order to do that, we must possess a mastery of the art of "coalitions", the art of "absorption" and the principles of "cooperation".

6-The necessity of achieving a union and balanced gradual merger between private work and public work:
We believe that what was written about this subject is many and is enough. But, it needs a time and a practical frame so that what is needed is achieved in a gradual and a balanced way that is compatible with the process of settlement.

7-The conviction that the success of the settlement of Islam and its

Movement in this country is a success to the global Islamic Movement and a true support for the sought-after state, God willing:

There is a conviction - with which this memorandum disagrees - that our focus in attempting to settle Islam in this country will lead to negligence in our duty towards the global Islamic Movement in supporting its project to establish the state. We believe that the reply is in two segments: One - The success of the Movement in America in establishing an observant Islamic base with power and effectiveness will be the best support and aid to the global Movement project. And the second - is the global Movement has not succeeded yet in "distributing roles" to its branches, stating what is the needed from them as one of the participants or contributors to the project to establish the global Islamic state. The day this happens, the children of the American Ikhwani branch will have far-reaching impact and positions that make the ancestors proud.

8-Absorbing Muslims and winning them with all of their factions and colors in America and Canada for the settlement project, and making it their cause, future and the basis of their Islamic life in this part of the world:

This issues requires from us to learn "the art of dealing with the others", as people are different and people in many colors. We need to adopt the principle which says, "Take from people... the best they have", their best specializations, experiences, arts, energies and abilities. By people here we mean those within or without the ranks of individuals and organizations. The policy of "taking" should be with what achieves the strategic goal and the settlement process. But the big challenge in front of us is: how to connect them all in "the orbit" of our plan and "the circle" of our Movement in order to achieve "the core" of our interest. To me, there is no choice for us other than alliance and mutual understanding of those who desire from our religion and those who agree from our belief in work. And the U.S. Islamic arena is full of those waiting...., the pioneers.

What matters is bringing people to the level of comprehension of the challenge that is facing us as Muslims in this country, conviction of our settlement project, and understanding the benefit of agreement, cooperation and alliance. At that time, if we ask for money, a lot of it would come, and if we ask for men, they would come in lines. What matters is that our plan is "the criterion and the balance" in our relationship with others.

Here, two points must be noted; the first one: we need to comprehend and understand the balance of the Islamic powers in the U.S. arena [and this might be the subject of a future study]. The second point: what we reached with the brothers in "ICNA" is considered a step in the right direction, the beginning of good and the first drop that requires growing and guidance.

9-Re-examining our organizational and administrative bodies, the type of leadership and the method of selecting it with what suits the challenges of the settlement mission:
The memorandum will be silent about details regarding this item even though it is logical and there is a lot to be said about it,

10-Growing and developing our resources and capabilities, our financial and human resources with what suits the magnitude of the grand mission:
If we examined the human and the financial resources the Ikhwan alone own in this country, we and others would feel proud and glorious. And if we add to them the resources of our friends and allies, those who circle in our orbit and those waiting on our banner, we would realize that we are able to open the door to settlement and walk through it seeking to make Almighty God's word the highest.

11-Utilizing the scientific method in planning, thinking and preparation of studies needed for the process of settlement:

Yes, we need this method, and we need many studies which aid in this civilization Jihadist operation. We will mention some of them briefly:

The history of the Islamic presence in America.
The history of the Islamic Ikhwani presence in America.
Islamic movements, organizations and organizations: analysis and criticism.
The phenomenon of the Islamic centers and schools: challenges, needs and statistics.
Islamic minorities.
Muslim and Arab communities.
The U.S. society: make-up and politics.
The U.S. society's view of Islam and Muslims... And many other studies which we can direct our brothers and allies to prepare, either through their academic studies or through their educational centers or organizational tasking. What is important is that we start.

12-Agreeing on a flexible, balanced and a clear "mechanism" to implement the process of settlement within a specific, gradual and balanced "time frame" that is in-line with the demands and challenges of the process of settlement.

13-Understanding the U.S. society from its different aspects an understanding that "qualifies" us to perform the mission of settling our Dawa' in its country "and growing it" on its land.

14-Adopting a written "jurisprudence" that includes legal and movement bases, principles, policies and interpretations which are suitable for the needs and challenges of the process of settlement.

15-Agreeing on "criteria" and balances to be a sort of "antennas" or "the watch tower" in order to make sure that all of our priorities, plans, programs, bodies, leadership, monies and activities march towards the process of the settlement.

16-Adopting a practical, flexible formula through which our central work complements our domestic work.

17-Understanding the role and the nature of work of "The Islamic Center" in every city with what achieves the goal of the process of settlement:
The center we seek is the one which constitutes the "axis" of our Movement, the "perimeter" of the circle of our work, our "balance center", the "base" for our rise and our "Dar al-Arqam" to educate us, prepare us and supply our battalions in addition to being the "niche" of our prayers.

This is in order for the Islamic center to turn - in action not in words - into a seed "for a small Islamic society" which is a reflection and a mirror to our central organizations. The center ought to turn into a "beehive" which produces sweet honey. Thus, the Islamic center would turn into a place for study, family, battalion, course, seminar, visit, sport, school, social club, women gathering, kindergarten for male and female youngsters, the office of the domestic political resolution, and the center for distributing our newspapers, magazines, books and our audio and visual tapes.

In brief we say: we would like for the Islamic center to become "The House of Dawa'" and "the general center" in deeds first before name. As much as we own and direct these centers at the continent level, we can say we are marching successfully towards the settlement of Dawa' in this country. Meaning that the "center's" role should be the same as the "mosque's" role during the time of God's prophet, God's prayers and peace be upon him, when he marched to "settle" the Dawa' in its first generation in Madina. from the mosque, he drew the Islamic life and provided to the world the most magnificent and fabulous civilization humanity knew. This mandates that, eventually, the region, the branch and the Usra turn into "operations rooms" for planning, direction, monitoring and leadership for the Islamic center in order to be a role model to be followed.

18-Adopting a system that is based on "selecting" workers, "role distribution" and "assigning" positions and responsibilities is based on specialization, desire and need with what achieves the process of settlement and contributes to its success.

19-Turning the principle of dedication for the Masuls of main positions within the Group into a rule, a basis and a policy in work. Without it, the process of settlement might be stalled [Talking about this point requires more details and discussion].

20-Understanding the importance of the "Organizational" shift in our Movement work, and doing Jihad in order to achieve it in the real world with what serves the process of settlement and expedites its results, God Almighty's willing:
The reason this paragraph was delayed is to stress its utmost importance as it constitutes the heart and the core of this memorandum. It also constitutes the practical aspect and the true measure of our success or failure in our march towards settlement. The talk about the organizations and the "organizational" mentality or phenomenon does not require much details. It suffices to say that the first pioneer of this phenomenon was our prophet Mohamed, God's peace, mercy and blessings be upon him, as he placed the foundation for the first civilized organization which is the mosque, which truly became "the comprehensive organization". And this was done by the pioneer of the contemporary Islamic Dawa', Imam martyr Hasan al-Banna, may God have mercy on him, when he and his brothers felt the

need to "re-establish" Islam and its movement anew, leading him to establish organizations with all their kinds: economic, social, media, scouting, professional and even the military ones. We must say that we are in a country which understands no language other than the language of the organizations, and one which does not respect or give weight to any group without effective, functional and strong organizations.

It is good fortune that there are brothers among us who have this "trend", mentality or inclination to build the organizations who have beat us by action and words which leads us to dare say honestly what Sadat in Egypt once said, "We want to build a country of organizations" - a word of right he meant wrong with. I say to my brothers, let us raise the banner of truth to establish right "We want to establish the Group of organizations", as without it we will not able to put our feet on the true path.

And in order for the process of settlement to be completed, we must plan and work from now to equip and prepare ourselves, our brothers, our apparatuses, our sections and our committees in order to turn into comprehensive organizations in a gradual and balanced way that is suitable with the need and the reality. What encourages us to do that - in addition to the aforementioned -is that we possess "seeds" for each organization from the organization we call for [See attachment number (1)].

All we need is to tweak them, coordinate their work, collect their elements and merge their efforts with others and then connect them with the comprehensive plan we seek.

For instance, We have a seed for a "comprehensive media and art" organization: we own a print + advanced typesetting machine + audio and visual center + art production office + magazines in Arabic and English [The Horizons, The Hope, The Politicians, Ha Falastine,

Press Clips, al-Zaytouna, Palestine Monitor, Social Sciences Magazines...] + art band + photographers + producers + programs anchors + journalists + in addition to other media and art experiences". Another example:

We have a seed for a "comprehensive Dawa' educational" organization: We have the Daw'a section in ISNA + Dr. Jamal Badawi Foundation + the center run by brother Hamed al-Ghazali + the Dawa' center the Dawa' Committee and brother Shaker al-Sayyed are seeking to establish now + in addition to other Daw'a efforts here and there...". And this applies to all the organizations we call on establishing.

The big challenge that is ahead of us is how to turn these seeds or "scattered" elements into comprehensive, stable, "settled" organizations that are connected with our Movement and which fly in our orbit and take orders from our guidance. This does not prevent - but calls for - each central organization to have its local branches but its connection with the Islamic center in the city is a must.

What is needed is to seek to prepare the atmosphere and the means to achieve "the merger" so that the sections, the committees, the regions, the branches and the Usras are eventually the heart and the core of these organizations.

Or, for the shift and the change to occur as follows:

1- The Movement Department + The Secretariat Department
2- Education Department + Dawa'a Com.
3- Sisters Department
4- The Financial Department + Investment Committee + The Endowment

5- Youth Department + Youths Organizations Department
6- The Social Committee + Matrimony Committee + Mercy Foundation
7- The Security Committee
8- The Political Depart. + Palestine Com.
9- The Group's Court + The Legal Com.
10- Domestic Work Department
11- Our magazines + the print + our art band
12- The Studies Association + The Publication House + Dar al-Kitab
13- Scientific and Medial societies
14- The Organizational Conference
15- The Shura Council + Planning Com.
16- The Executive Office
17- The General Masul
18- The regions, branches & Usras

The Organizational & Administrative Organization -The General Center
Dawa' and Educational Organization
The Women's Organization
The Economic Organization
Youth Organizations
The Social Organization
The Security Organization
The Political Organization
The Judicial Organization
Its work is to be distributed to the rest of the organizations
The Media and Art Organization
The Intellectual & Cultural
Scientific, Educational & Professional Organization

The Islamic-American Founding Conference
The Shura Council for the Islamic-American Movement
The Executive Office of the Islamic-American Movement
Chairman of the Islamic Movement and its official Spokesman
Field leaders of organizations & Islamic centers

Five: Comprehensive Settlement Organization:
We would then seek and struggle in order to make each one of these above-mentioned organizations a "comprehensive organization" throughout the days and the years, and as long as we are destined to be in this country. What is important is that we put the foundation and we will be followed by peoples and generations that would finish the march and the road but with a clearly-defined guidance.

And, in order for us to clarify what we mean with the comprehensive, specialized organization, we mention here the characteristics and traits of each organization of the "promising" organizations.

1-From the Dawa' and educational aspect [The Dawa* and Educational Organization]: to
include:
The Organization to spread the Dawa' (Central and local branches).
An institute to graduate Callers and Educators.
Scholars, Callers, Educators, Preachers and Program Anchors.
Art and communication technology, Conveyance and Dawa'.
A television station.
A specialized Dawa' magazine.
A radio station.
The Higher Islamic Council for Callers and Educators.
The Higher Council for Mosques and Islamic Centers.
Friendship Societies with the other religions... and things like that.

108

2-Politically [The Political Organization]: to include:
A central political party.
Local political offices.
Political symbols.
Relationships and alliances.
The American Organization for Islamic Political Action
Advanced Information Centers....and things like that.

3-Media [The Media and Art Organization]: to include:
A daily newspaper,
Weekly, monthly and seasonal magazines.
Radio stations.
Television programs.
Audio and visual centers.
A magazine for the Muslim child.
A magazine for the Muslim woman.
A print and typesetting machines.
A production office.
A photography and recording studio
Art bands for acting, chanting and theater.
A marketing and art production office... and things like that.

4-Economically [The Economic Organization!: to include:An Islamic
Central bank.
Islamic endowments.
Investment projects.
An organization for interest-free loans.... and things like that.

**5-Scientifically and Professionally [The Scientific. Educational
and Professional Organization]:** to include:

Scientific research centers.

Technical organizations and vocational training.

An Islamic university.

Islamic schools.

A council for education and scientific research.

Centers to train teachers.

Scientific societies in schools.

An office for academic guidance.

A body for authorship and Islamic curricula.... and things like that.

6-Culturally and Intellectually [The Cultural and Intellectual Organization]: to include:

A center for studies and research.

Cultural and intellectual foundations such as [The Social Scientists Society - Scientists and Engineers Society....].

An organization for Islamic thought and culture.

A publication, translation and distribution house for Islamic books.

An office for archiving, history and authentication

The project to translate the Noble Quran, the Noble Sayings....and things like that.

7-Socially [The Social-Charitable Organization]: to include:

Social clubs for the youths and the community's sons and daughters

Local societies for social welfare and the services are tied to the Islamic centers

The Islamic Organization to Combat the Social Ills of the U.S. Society

Islamic houses project

Matrimony and family cases office....and things like that.

8-Youths [The Youth Organization!: to include:

Central and local youths foundations.
Sports teams and clubs
Scouting teams....and things like that.

9-Women [The Women Organization]: to include:

Central and local women societies.
Organizations of training, vocational and housekeeping.
An organization to train female preachers.
Islamic kindergartens...and things like that.

10-Organizationally and Administratively [The Administrative and Organizational Organization!: to include:
An institute for training, growth, development and planning
Prominent experts in this field
Work systems, bylaws and charters fit for running the most complicated bodies and organizations
A periodic magazine in Islamic development and administration.
Owning camps and halls for the various activities.
A data, polling and census bank.
An advanced communication network.
An advanced archive for our heritage and production....and things like that.

11-Security [The Security Organization!: to include:
Clubs for training and learning self-defense techniques.
A center which is concerned with the security issues [Technical, intellectual, technological and human]....and things like that.

12-Legally [The Legal Organization]: to include:
A Central Jurisprudence Council.
A Central Islamic Court.

Muslim Attorneys Society.
The Islamic Foundation for Defense of Muslims' Rights...and
things like that. And success is by God.

Attachment

A list of our organizations and the organizations of our friends
[Imagine if t they all march according to one plan!!!]

ISNA   ISLAMIC SOCIETY OF NORTH AMERICA

MSA   MUSLIM STUDENTS' ASSOCIATION

MCA   THE MUSLIM COMMUNITIES ASSOCIATION

AMSS   THE ASSOCIATION OF MUSLIM SOCIAL SCIENTISTS

AMSE   THE ASSOCIATION OF MUSLIM SCIENTISTS AND ENGINEERS

IMA   ISLAMIC MEDICAL ASSOCIATION

ITC   ISLAMIC TEACHING CENTER

NAIT   NORTH AMERICAN ISLAMIC TRUST

FID   FOUNDATION FOR INTERNATIONAL DEVELOMENT

IHC   ISLAMIC HOUSING COOPERATIVE

ICD   ISLAMIC CENTERS DIVISION

ATP   AMERICAN TRUST PUBLICATIONS

AVC   AUDIO-VISUAL CENTER

IBS   ISLAMIC BOOK SERVICE

MBA   MUSLIM BUSINESSMEN ASSOCIATION

MYNA   MUSLIM YOUTH OF NORTH AMERICA

IFC   ISNA FIQH COMMITTEE

IPAC   ISNA POLITICAL AWARENESS COMMITTEE

IED   ISLAMIC EDUCATION DEPARTMENT

MAYA   MUSLIM ARAB YOUTH ASSOCIATION

MISG   MALASIAN ISLAMIC STUDY GROUP

IAP	ISLAMIC ASSOCIATION FOR PALESTINE
UASR	UNITED ASSOCIATION FOR STUDIES AND RESEARCH
OLF	OCCUPIED LAND FUND
MIA	MERCEY INTERNATIONAL ASSOCIATION
ICNA	ISLAMIC CIRCLE OF NORTH AMERICA
BMI	BA1TUL MAL INC
IIIT	INTERNATIONAL INSTITUTE FOR ISLAMIC THOUGHT
IIC	ISLAMIC INFORMATION CENTER

How far has the Muslim Brotherhood advanced with their plan of their 'Third' and 'Silent' Jihad? That will be discussed in the next chapter.

Chapter 5

Muslim Brotherhood Infiltration

How far have they come? The following information shows their progress within the confines of Agenda 21, Social Justice, and the Muslim Brotherhood agenda.

The following information shows the supporting agenda of the Muslim Brotherhood and Agenda 21 by our government. Many influential Muslims have already been appointed to high political leadership and advisory roles in our government. This includes four at the very top. Their positions might have changed since the information was posted; nevertheless it demonstrates the strategic positions these individuals have occupied or are now occupying:

Arif Alikhan (From Wikipedia)

"Arif Alikhan" was the Deputy Executive Director for Homeland Security, Law Enforcement, and Fire/EMS at Los Angeles World

Airports. He was appointed to the new position in October 2011 and is responsible for the 1,200 sworn police officers and civilian security officers that protect Los Angeles International Airport, Ontario International Airport, and Van Nuys Airport. He is also responsible for all fire and emergency medical services at LAWA's three airports. Alikhan is a former Distinguished Professor of Homeland Security and Counterterrorism at the National Defense University (NDU), College of International Security Affairs in Washington, D.C. He teaches and lectures on a variety subjects involving homeland and national security issues for U.S. military and civilian security professionals and is a recognized expert on U.S. government homeland security and counter terrorism policies.

Alikhan was appointed to the Obama Administration in 2009 as Assistant Secretary for Policy Development at the United States Department of Homeland Security. He is also a former Deputy Mayor of Homeland Security and Public Safety for the City of Los Angeles, former federal prosecutor with the United States Attorneys Office in Los Angeles, and a former senior adviser to Attorneys General John Ashcroft and Alberto Gonzales while serving at the Department of Justice in Washington, D.C. He no longer works for the government.

Mohammed Elibiary, Homeland Security Adviser
(Reported by Jordan Schachtel at Brietbart.com)

Mohamed Elibiary is a senior member of the Department of Homeland Security Advisory Council. According to a report by the Center for Security Policy, Elibiary also supports brokering a U.S. partnership with the Muslim Brotherhood terrorist group.

This week, Breitbart's Kerry Picket reported that Elibiary wrote on Twitter that it is "inevitable that the Caliphate returns."

Under an Islamic caliphate, all citizens would be forced to comply with the highly oppressive Islamic Sharia law.

Weasel Zippers reported Wednesday that ISIS is now flooding social media sites using DHS advisor Elibiary's "inevitable caliphate" comments, hoping to use Elibiary's words as a recruiting tool to add more militants to their jihadi personnel.

Elibiary was seemingly indifferent towards the caliphate-seeking tactics of the ruthless terrorist group known as Islamic State of Iraq and al-Sham (ISIS), which is marching through Iraq slaughtering non-Sunni Muslims and beheading innocents. He said on Twitter, "Kind of comical watching pundits on some US TV channels freak out about an #ISIS #Caliphate." He continued, "Easy folks, take deep breath & relax. #Iraq."

At first glance, Elibiary's resume implies that he is the perfect candidate for the post at which he serves. He was a founder of the Texas-based intelligence firm, Lonestar. Elibiary's CV shows that he has advised governments on local, state, and federal levels. He was even awarded one of the top civilian prizes from the Federal Bureau of Investigation for "combating extremism."

However, questions remain about how Elibiary attained his counterterrorism knowledge. According to Judicial Watch, a long-time friend of Elibiary, Shukri Abu Baker, was the former president of the Holy Land Foundation, a group founded as a financing operation for the Muslim Brotherhood terrorist group Hamas. Baker and three others were sentenced to 65 years in prison for using the Holy Land Foundation to finance Hamas' primary mission: the destruction of the State of Israel. The FBI wiretapped Baker as he told his fellow foundation members to be as deceptive as possible to get their message across. According to national security expert Ryan Mauro, he would frequently tell them, "War is deception."

The Holy Land Foundation trial was the biggest terror-financing trial in the history of the United States. Former federal prosecutor Andy McCarthy described the HLF as "the piggy bank set up by the Brotherhood in the U.S., under the guise of 'charity,' to fund Hamas to the tune of tens of millions of dollars during the deadly intifada."

In 2004, Elibiary was a speaker at an event called "A Tribute to the Great Islamic Visionary," which honored the ruthless theocratic Iranian Ayatollah Khomeini.

In 2006, Elibiary penned an op-ed stating that everyone should read Sayyid Qutb, who is a man widely seen as the founder of radical Islamic groups like Al Qaeda and the Muslim Brotherhood. Elibiary wrote, "I'd recommend everyone read Qutb, but read him with an eye to improving America not just to be jealous with malice in our hearts."

In 2011, evidence surfaced that Texas authorities caught Elibiary downloading classified information to his personal computer and sending it to the media in an effort to smear Texas Governor Rick Perry as an 'Islamophobe.' On October 26, 2011, when Congressman Louie Gohmert asked Former DHS Secretary Janet Napolitano about the allegations, she said that she was not aware of them. A few months later, Gohmert would again bring up Elibiary's misdeeds. Napolitano refused to acknowledge the report, saying the statements were "false, misleading, objectionable, and wrong." The DHS Secretary never answered the accusations, but she did express that "Muslims have been helping DHS for a long time."

In 2013, Elibiary declared that his friend Baker, the man who was caught financing terrorist group Hamas, was simply a victim of political persecution because he happened to be a Muslim.

Rashad Hussain, (From Wikipedia)

Rashad Hussain (born in 1978), is an American attorney, and U.S. Special Envoy to the Organization of Islamic Cooperation (OIC), the second largest intergovernmental body after the UN, with 57 member states. Hussain, a Muslim of Indian heritage, has served in the White House Counsel's Office and on the National Security Council, and in his role as Envoy, has advised the Administration on policy issues related to the Muslim world. He has traveled to numerous countries and international conferences, and has met with foreign leaders and Muslims around the world. His position, "a kind of ambassador at large to Muslim countries," was created by President George W. Bush.

Salam al-Marayati, Obama Adviser and founder of the Muslim Public Affairs Council and is its current executive director. (From Investigativeproject.org: Apologists or Extremists.)

A founder of the Muslim Public Affairs Council and its current executive director, Salam al-Marayati's family moved to the United States from Iraq when he was a young boy. He gained national attention in 1999, when then-House Democratic Leader Richard Gephardt nominated him to serve on the National Commission on Terrorism. Gephardt later withdrew the nomination after a public backlash highlighted al-Marayati's defense of terrorist acts and the groups who carry them out.

Al-Marayati's record on defending terrorist groups and extremists is substantial. During a 2002 speech at the State Department, Salam al-Marayati, said, "Rashid Ghannouchi is an example of those who promote this need for dialogue between civilizations, not confrontation." Ghannoushi was the head of Tunisia's banned Muslim Brotherhood-aligned Al-Nahda Party and was convicted by a Tunisian court of responsibility for a bomb blast that blew the foot off a British tourist.

In a 1999 PBS interview, he called Hizballah attacks "legitimate resistance," but later added "when a Muslim commits an act of terrorism, we stand very loudly and clearly against that Muslim that committed that act of violence."

Yet in 1996, he issued no condemnation for a man who crashed his car into a crowded Jerusalem bus stop, shouting Allahu Akbar. One person was killed and 23 others injured in the incident. The attacker was shot dead at the scene, something al-Marayati condemned as a "provocative act" and he called for the shooter's extradition to the United States to stand trial.

Al-Marayati has continued to attempt to minimize terrorist attacks by Muslims, decry U.S. government anti-terrorism measures, and blame anything he can on the state of Israel. For instance, on September 11,

2001, on a Los Angeles radio program al-Marayati said, "If we're going to look at suspects, we should look to the groups that benefit the most from these kinds of incidents, and I think we should put the state of Israel on the suspect list because I think this diverts attention from what's happening in the Palestinian territories so that they can go on with their aggression and occupation and apartheid policies."

Two years later, in a March 2003 Los Angeles Times article, Salam al-Marayati blasted the FBI, stating that they had been targeting people on the basis of race and religion. Ignoring several prominent terrorism cases across the country, he added, "That's what they've been doing since the attacks, and we don't know of any case that has resulted in the arrest, indictment or prosecution of a terrorist."

Commenting on the government's actions against alleged terrorist financiers, specifically of Rafil Dhafir of Help the Needy (indicted in February 2003, convicted and sentenced to 22 years in prison in 2005) and his cohorts, in October 2004, Salam al-Marayati said, "It is a sham. You just hope at the end of a long battle these people can be vindicated because they did nothing wrong."

In response to the government's recent refusal to grant MPAC's request to release Holy Land Foundation, Benevolence International Foundation, and Global Relief Foundation funds to a third-party, al-Marayati asserted, in 2004, that "the government…betrayed us."

At a fundraising dinner for Palestinian Islamic Jihad member Sami Al-Arian in Anaheim, California in 2006, al-Marayati said to the attendees, "So if we have this case where we are being dictated upon, not only on terminology, but dictated upon on who speaks for us, and our organizations, our charities, are shut down one by one. Therefore, brothers and sisters, there is a storm that is coming. That storm is going to be worse than Japanese internment."

Beyond the effect these words may have in causing hysteria, distrust, and fear in the Muslim-American community, al-Marayati has advised Muslims to shun FBI efforts to recruit informants. Speaking to an audience in Dallas in 2005, he stated, "We reject any efforts, notion, suggestion that Muslim should start spying on one another. In fact if you look at the Lodi case, the disaster of Lodi is that Muslims were reporting each other to the authorities saying, 'Oh, this person is an extremist' and the other camp saying the same things so both of them got in trouble. So, we are, this is the model not to follow."

MPAC, meanwhile, has issued policy papers which argue for the removal of Hizballah and Hamas from U.S. terrorist designations. The 1999 counter-terrorism "policy paper" asks "…is Lebanon's Hezbollah, which calls for the creation of an Islamic republic, a terrorist organization? Again, most of its members are not actively involved in terror."

It then tries to minimize Hizballah's brutal attack on the U.S. Marine barracks in Lebanon in 1983 -- an attack which killed 241 U.S. military personnel:

"…this attack, for all the pain it caused, was not in a strict sense, a terrorist operation. It was a military operation, producing no civilian casualties -- exactly the kind of attack that Americans might have lauded had it been directed against Washington's enemies."

The 2003 counter-terrorism paper advocated removing Hamas, Palestinian Islamic Jihad and Hizballah from the federal government's list of designated terrorist groups. It reads:

"Meanwhile, Arab states question Washington's list of designated pro-Palestinian groups and humanitarian organizations. It is clear that the current terrorist threat to the US emanates from Al-Qaeda and not Palestinian groups. There is no evidence that Palestinian groups designated as terrorist organizations have any connections to Al-Qaeda. Yet the preoccupation with these groups raises the question as to whether targeting Palestinian groups serves true national security interests or is based on political considerations."

Imam Mohamed Magid, Obama's Sharia Czar from the Islamic Society of North America (ISNA.) (From Counterjihadreport.com - by John Guandolo)

Over the last several years, the presence of Muslim Brotherhood (MB) operatives working inside the federal government advising our senior leaders has been definitively documented. This penetration of our system is shocking and constitutes an immediate danger for American citizens. The success of the MB's influence operation from within our government is now manifesting itself with national and global implications for the security of America and its citizens.

In July of this year, the CIA hosted a 2-day training program at its headquarters in Langley, Virginia entitled "Countering Violent Extremism Workshop for the National Capitol Region."

Present at this conference were local, state, and federal officials from nearly every law enforcement, military, and intelligence organization around the Washington Metropolitan area. In addition to the senior CIA, FBI, and DHS officials conducting the training, members of the Muslim community moderated and led the training throughout the 2-day program. Notable among these was Imam Mohammed Magid who participated in speaking about "Building Communities of Trust: A Local Example of a Partnership between the All Dulles Area Muslim Society (ADAMS) and Law Enforcement."

How was Imam Magid vetted to speak at CIA Headquarters? And who vetted him?

The ADAMS Center is a Muslim Brotherhood front organization. It was founded by some of the most senior Muslim Brothers in the United States, to include Ahmed Totanji, who still resides in Herndon, Virginia. Its website proclaims "[ADAMS] is a membership organization registered in the State of Virginia as a non-profit, tax exempt corporation and is affiliated with the Islamic Society of North America (ISNA)."

Imam Magid is the Executive Director of the ADAMS Center. He is also the President of the Islamic Society of North America (ISNA), the largest Muslim Brotherhood organization in the U.S. which was found to be a financial support entity for Hamas in the largest terrorism financing and Hamas trial in U.S. history (US v Holy Land Foundation, Dallas, 2008). Having Magid advise and teach U.S. intelligence and law enforcement officials can only be aptly described as insane. According to officials at Langley who were willing to speak on the condition of anonymity, this is an outrage – but none of the leaders on the inside seem to understand the gravity of this threat. To say the fox is in the hen house would be an understatement.

Eboo Patel, Advisory Council on Faith-Based Neighborhood Partnerships. (From discoverthenetworks.org)

He has ties to Bill Ayers, Bernardine Dohrn, Rashid Khalidi, Mumia Abu-Jamal, and Imam Feisal Abdul Rauf;

Was appointed to President Barack Obama's Advisory Council on Faith-Based Neighborhood Partnerships in 2009;

Describes the revolutionary communist Van Jones as an "American patriot," a "faith hero," and one of "the true giants of history."

Born November 9, 1975 in Mumbai, India, Eboo Patel was raised in Glen Ellyn, Illinois. After earning a bachelor's degree in sociology from the University of Illinois at Urbana-Champaign, he taught at an alternative-education program for high-school dropouts in Chicago and, inspired by Dorothy Day's Catholic Worker Movement, established a cooperative living community for activists and artists in Chicago's Uptown area.

Patel, a Muslim, went on to earn a doctorate in the sociology of religion from Oxford University. During his Oxford years, he ran interfaith youth projects in India, Sri Lanka, and South Africa. In 2002 Patel and a Jewish friend co-founded, with the help of a $35,000 grant from the Ford Foundation, the Chicago-based InterFaith Youth Corps (IFYC) as a forum where "service" could be used as a "bridge" to unite "young people from different faiths." Patel remains IFYC's executive director to this day.

In 2005 Patel and several young radicals co-authored the book Letters from Young Activists: Today's Rebels Speak Out. Among Patel's co-authors were Chesa Boudin (the adopted son of former Weather Underground terrorist Bill Ayers) and Ismail Khalidi (the son of Columbia University professor Rashid Khalidi). The book's Preface was written by Ayers' wife, Weather Underground co-founder Bernardine Dohrn. The back cover featured an endorsement from the convicted cop-killer and former Black Panther Party member Mumia Abu-Jamal. And on the Acknowledgments page, Patel and his fellow authors thanked Ayers personally for the "guidance" and "encouragement" he had provided.

In 2006 Patel published Building the Interfaith Youth Movement: Beyond Dialogue to Action. The book's Afterword was written by Imam Feisal Abdul Rauf, famous for having led an effort to construct a large mosque near the site of the 9/11 attacks in Manhattan.

In Patel's 2007 book, Saving Each Other, Saving Ourselves, the author recounts discussions that he had with Imam Rauf regarding the future of Islam in the United States. "Islam is a religion that has always been revitalized by its migration," writes Patel. "America is a nation that has been constantly rejuvenated by immigrants. There is now a critical mass of Muslims in America." The website of the American Society for Muslim Advancement, an organization co-founded by Rauf, once listed Patel as one of the top "Muslim Leaders of Tomorrow."

In a 2007 interview with National Public Radio to promote his next newly published book, Acts of Faith, Patel was asked about the "affinity" he felt for the radicalism of Bill Ayers, as he described in the book. Noting that "I actually grew up in the same hometown that Bill

Ayers did," Patel replied: "I was kind of taught the same myths about America, a land of freedom and equality and justice, etc., etc. And then, when I got to college, I saw people eating out of garbage cans for dinner, and I saw Vietnam vets drinking mouthwash for the alcohol, and I thought to myself, this is not the myth that I grew up with." This harsh reality, Patel said, caused him to feel enormous "rage," and he credited the "faith-based movement" for having helped him "direct that rage in a direction far more compassionate and far more merciful—with the Catholic Worker Movement." "Had I been one of the people involved in the Weather Underground who were sitting at my kitchen table when I was 18 years old and raging," said Patel, "my life could have been very different."

In a June 2008 interview with the leftist evangelical ministry Sojourners, Patel reiterated the sense of rage he had felt upon realizing that "everything you were taught was wrong—about fairness, about equality, about Christopher Columbus, about Thomas Jefferson." He elaborated that the faith movement had given him a "way to have a radical view of the world—radical equality, radical peace, radical possibility—that is love-based, not anger-based."

In February 2009, Patel was appointed to President Barack Obama's Advisory Council on Faith-Based Neighborhood Partnerships.

In an October 2009 article in Newtopia magazine, a liberal cultural publication, Patel asserted that "Muslim totalitarians" were not all that different from "the Christian totalitarians in America," "the Jewish totalitarians in Israel," or "the Hindu totalitarians in India."

In late July 2011, Patel spoke at the main event of a three-day convention held by the Muslim Students Association. Specifically, he participated in a panel alongside Tariq Ramadan (grandson of Muslim Brotherhood founder Hasan al-Banna) and Siraj Wahhaj (who was named as a possible co-conspirator in the 1993 World Trade Center bombing).

In 2011 Patel depicted Van Jones, the revolutionary communist who had served several months as President Obama's "green jobs" czar, as an "American patriot," a "faith hero," and one of "the true giants of history."

Patel is a regular contributor to the Washington Post, National Public Radio, and CNN. He has blogged for the Huffington Post, USA Today, and Sojourners, among other outlets. Moreover, he has served on the Council on Foreign Relations' religious advisory committee, the Aga Khan Foundation's national committee, and the Duke University Islamic Studies Center's advisory board. He is a fellow of the Ashoka Foundation, and has spoken in such major venues as the Clinton Global Initiative and the Nobel Peace Prize Forum. End of article.

Do you wonder why Barack Obama is such a big supporter of the Muslim Brotherhood? Why did he once bow down to a powerful Muslim leader? Why does he have many in his administration as 'senior advisors?' Why does he let them advance, ignores their actions, while he tries to improve his golf game? Is our great country in great danger from his actions to continue the war on Christians? What are his real connections to the Muslim Brotherhood? His actions seem directly connected to their 'Strategic Plan.'

One of the first actions to begin their Islamic Strategic Plan, not protested by Obama or any others in his administration, was to infiltrate and begin their indoctrination in America's education system. The following article explains some examples of that process. There are many more - too many to identify and explain in this short book.

This is an article from sfgate.com, titled: 'Islam in America's public schools: Education or indoctrination?' It was written by Cinnamon Stillwell and published Wednesday, June 11, 2008:

"With fatal terrorist attacks on the decline worldwide and al Qaeda apparently in disarray, it would seem a time for optimism in the global war on terrorism. But the war has simply shifted to a different arena. Islamists, or those who believe that Islam is a political and religious system that must dominate all others, are focusing less on the military and more on the ideological. It turns out that Western liberal democracies can be subverted without firing a shot.

Nowhere is this more evident than in the educational realm. Islamists have taken what's come to be known as the "soft jihad" into America's classrooms and children in K-12 are the first casualties. Whether it is textbooks, curriculum, classroom exercises, film screenings, speakers or teacher training, public education in America is under assault.

Capitalizing on the post-9/11 demand for Arabic instruction, some public, charter and voucher-funded private schools are inappropriately using taxpayer dollars to implement a religious curriculum. They are also bringing in outside speakers with Islamist ties or sympathies. As a result, not only are children receiving a biased education, but possible violations of the First Amendment's Establishment Clause abound. Consider the following cases:

Last month, students at Friendswood Junior High in Houston were required to attend an "Islamic Awareness" presentation during class time allotted for physical education. The presentation involved two representatives from the Council on American-Islamic Relations, an organization with a record of Islamist statements and terrorism convictions. According to students, they were taught that "there is one God, his name is Allah" and that "Adam, Noah and Jesus are prophets." Students were also taught about the Five Pillars of Islam and how to pray five times a day and wear Islamic religious garb. Parents were not notified about the presentation and it wasn't until a number of complaints arose that school officials responded with an apologetic e-mail.

Earlier this year at Lake Brantley High School in Seminole County, Fla., speakers from the Academy for Learning Islam gave a presentation to students about "cultural diversity" that extended to a detailed discussion of the Quran and Islam. The school neither screened the ALI speakers nor notified parents. After a number of complaints, local media coverage and a subsequent investigation, the school district apologized for the inappropriate presentation, admitting that it violated the law. Subsequently, ALI was removed from the Seminole County school system's Dividends and Speaker's Bureau.

As reported by the Cabinet Press, a school project last year at Amherst Middle School transformed "the quaint colonial town of Amherst, N.H., into a Saudi Arabian Bedouin tent community." Male and female students were segregated, with the girls hosting "hijab and veil stations" and handing out the oppressive head-to-toe black garment known as the abaya to female guests. Meanwhile, the boys hosted food and Arabic dancing stations because, as explained in the article, "the traditions of Saudi Arabia at this time prevent women from participating in these public roles." An "Islamic religion station" offered up a prayer rug, verses from the Quran, prayer items and a compass pointed towards Mecca. The fact that female subjugation was presented as a benign cultural practice and Islamic religious rituals were promoted with public funds is cause for concern.

Tarek ibn Ziyad Academy, a charter school in Inver Grove Heights, Minn., came under recent scrutiny after Minneapolis Star-Tribune columnist Katherine Kersten brought to light concerns about public funding for its overtly religious curriculum. The school is housed in the Muslim American Society's (the American branch of the Egyptian Islamist group the Muslim Brotherhood) Minnesota building, alongside a mosque, and the daily routine includes prayer, ritual washing, halal food preparation and an after-school "Islamic studies" program. Kersten's columns prompted the Minnesota chapter of the American Civil Liberties Union to issue a press release expressing its own reservations about potential First Amendment violations. An investigation initiated by the Minnesota Department of Education verified several of Kersten's allegations and the school has since promised to make the appropriate changes. In a bizarre twist, when a local television news crew tried to report on the findings from school grounds, school officials confronted them and wrestled a camera away from one of its photographers, injuring him in the process.

The controversy surrounding the founding of New York City's Arabic language public school, Khalil Gibran International Academy, last year continues. Former principal Dhabah "Debbie" Almontaser was asked to step down after publicly defending T-shirts produced by Arab Women Active in the Arts and Media, an organization with whom she shared office space, emblazoned with "Intifada NYC." But KGIA has other troublesome associations. Its advisory board includes three imams, one of whom, New York University Imam Khalid Latif, sent a threatening letter to the university's president regarding a planned display of the Danish cartoons. Another, Shamsi Ali, runs the Jamaica Muslim Center Quranic Memorization School in Queens, a replica of the type of Pakistani madrassa (or school) counter-terrorism officials have been warning about since 9/11. Accordingly, several parents founded Stop the Madrassa: A Community Coalition to voice their contention that KGIA is an inappropriate candidate for taxpayer funding. End of article.

The war on Christians in the U.S. has many strategies and tactics. Another is described in the next chapter.

Chapter 6

War in the U.S.

Although the war against God and Christians started insidiously during the 1960s and 1970s, our proclaimed version started openly with statements by influential leaders such as Barack Obama. They threw trite comments and innuendoes into their speeches when the subject allowed them to do so. Since Barack Obama became president, his subtle attacks against Christianity is more consistently documented. He began his open and vocal attacks in 2006.

On June 28, 2006, during his 'Call to Renewal' speech, he mocked three sections of the Bible, including the Sermon on the Mount, which he called 'so radical.' He asked, mockingly, "Can either of these be used to guide public policy?" This is part of his speech most often quoted, in parts:

"Moreover, given the increasing diversity of America's population, the dangers of sectarianism have never been greater. Whatever we once were, we are no longer just a Christian nation; we are also a Jewish nation, a Muslim nation, a Buddhist nation, a Hindu nation, and a nation of nonbelievers.

And even if we did have only Christians in our midst, if we expelled every non-Christian from the United States of America, whose Christianity would we teach in the schools? Would we go with James Dobson's, or Al Sharpton's? Which passages of Scripture should guide our public policy? Should we go with Leviticus, which suggests slavery is ok and that eating shellfish is abomination? How about Deuteronomy, which suggests stoning your child if he strays from the faith? Or should we just stick to the Sermon on the Mount - a passage that is so radical that it's doubtful that our own Defense Department would survive its application? So before we get carried away, let's read our bibles. Folks haven't been reading their bibles."

Those who listened to the spoken version of this speech heard him say, "We are no longer a Christian nation." Then he interjected the "not just" comment after that. What was his thinking during that correction? Was it a simple slip, or was he judging his audience to decide if the "not just" comment should be applied or deleted? His later war on Christian principles might suggest he really meant "We are no longer a Christian nation."

On April 16, 2009, he required the monogram for the name of Jesus be covered before he made his speech at Georgetown University. The monogram above an archway was covered with black painted plywood. Certainly he would not consider this blasphemy or an attack on Christianity - black painted plywood covering the symbol of Jesus. This is a summary of that event reported by CNSNews.com:

"Amidst all of the American flags and presidential seals, there was something missing when President Barack Obama gave an economic speech at Georgetown University this week -- Jesus. The White House asked Georgetown to cover a monogram symbolizing Jesus' name in Gaston Hall, which Obama used for his speech, according to CNSNews.com. The gold "IHS" monogram inscribed on a pediment in the hall was covered over by a piece of black-painted plywood, and remained covered over the next day, CNSNews.com reported.

The Washington Times' Belief Blog asked the university about the presidential request: While the "IHS" directly behind where Obama spoke was covered over, CNSNews.com said the monogram was still visible in 26 other places in the hall during his speech. Those areas just weren't as prominent. The Belief Blog talked with the Rev. Thomas Reese, a senior fellow at the Woodstock Institute at Georgetown University, who said he didn't think "this is motivated by theology, but by communications strategy."

The blog also talked with Catholic University spokesman Victor Nakas, who felt a bit more strongly on the subject: "I can't imagine, as the bishops' university and the national university of the Catholic Church, that we would ever cover up our religious art or signage for any reason," Mr. Nakas wrote. "Our Catholic faith is integral to our identity as an institution of higher education."

Should this covering of the symbol of Jesus be considered another 'denial?' Perhaps Obama has set a new record. Peter denied Jesus only three times. Perhaps Obama and his close followers know no limit to the number of times they will deny Jesus and insult and disavow Christianity. Under this environment of anti-Christian actions and examples, many other actions of war against Christians routinely continue to occur. Following are seven clear and recent examples reported by John Hawkins at Townhall.com. The article published September 17, 2013 is titled: '7 Examples of Discrimination Against Christians in America.'

7 Examples of Discrimination Against Christians in America.

"The majority of Americans are Christians, but we're not treated with respect by the culture, the schools, or by our politicians. "Vengeance" may be the Lord's to dish out, but that doesn't mean Christians have to support the people who are attacking us or meekly stand by when other followers of Christ are denigrated and oppressed for their faith. The habitual wimpiness of so many Christians is particularly grating because when Christians shine a spotlight on these attacks and say, "That's enough," more often than not we win. So, if Christians across the country were consistently willing to speak out and take action, you'd be surprised at how quickly our culture would begin to change. If that happens, instead of seeing this many incidents every year (All of these happened in 2013), they'd be a once in a blue moon occurrence:

1) Florida Ministry Told To Choose Between Jesus And Helping The Poor:"For the past 31 years, the Christian ministry has been providing food to the hungry in Lake City, Fla. without any problems. But all that changed when they said a state government worker showed up to negotiate a new contract. ...(A) state agriculture department official told them they would not be allowed to receive USDA food unless they removed portraits of Christ, the Ten Commandments, a banner that read 'Jesus is Lord' and stopping giving Bibles to the needy."

When the government tells the Christian Service Center it has to give up on Christ or quit using USDA food to help the poor, that's religious discrimination.

2) Billy Graham Evangelistic Association: Obama's IRS Was "Targeting and Attempting to Intimidate Us:"It's well known that the IRS targeted Obama's political enemies in the Tea Party, but the IRS also targeted his Christian enemies in the Billy Graham Evangelistic Association.

Franklin Graham, the president of the Billy Graham Evangelistic Association and the family's international humanitarian organization Samaritan's Purse, said that the IRS notified the organizations in September that it was conducting a "review" of their activities for tax year 2010.

"While these audits not only wasted taxpayer money, they wasted money contributed by donors for ministry purposes as we had to spend precious resources servicing the IRS agents in our offices," Graham wrote in the letter, which was shared with POLITICO. "I believe that someone in the administration was targeting and attempting to intimidate us. This is morally wrong and unethical – indeed some would call it 'un-American.'"

Graham said that "in light" of the IRS admission that it targeted Tea party groups for added scrutiny, "I do not believe that the IRS audit of our two organizations last year is a coincidence – or justifiable."

The IRS would certainly deny targeting Graham's group because it's a Christian organization, but of course, the IRS would deny that it targeted the Tea Party groups for political reasons as well.

3) California Christians Found "Not Guilty" of Reading Bible Near Government Offices:"A court has said that a pair of Christians were 'allowed' to read the Bible aloud outside the Department of Motor Vehicles in Hemet, California. Wasn't it kind of the government courts in California to say that these Christians were allowed to have their rights to free religious expression? ...Back in 2011 Mark Mackey and Bret Coronado were arrested and charged with misdemeanor offenses for reading the Bible outside the DMV location. ... But on August 13, Superior Court Judge Timothy Freer found the men 'not guilty' of any offenses. ...Interestingly, the judge also pointed out that the law prosecutors tried to invoke was likely unconstitutional as it gave law enforcement overbroad powers to quash public gatherings in the first place. Sadly, this case did not go toward settling the constitutionality of the law, but it was a victory of sorts to have the judge even mention the fact."

Yes, there were actually Americans arrested for reading the Bible on public property. What do you think the chances are that two Muslims reading the Quran would have been arrested under the same circumstances?

4) Colorado Baker Faces Year In Jail For Refusing To Make Cake For Gay Wedding: You can support gay marriage or you can be Christian, but you can't do both. You can pretend to do both, but you're giving up your Christian beliefs to be more palatable to people who are hostile to Christianity. The folks at Masterpiece Cakeshop simply declined to make a cake for a gay wedding because it conflicted with their Christian beliefs. They learned that's now illegal.

According to attorney Nicolle Martin, the owners of a Colorado bakery could face a year in prison for refusing to make a cake for a gay wedding, Jim Hoft reported at the Gateway Pundit Monday.

"The complainants can sue him civilly in the regular courts system or he can potentially be prosecuted by the district attorney for up to twelve months in jail," Martin told Hoft.

In June, the Advocate said the Colorado Attorney General's office filed a discrimination complaint against the owners of Masterpiece Cakeshop in Denver after the bakers refused to bake a cake for Dave Mullins and Charlie Craig, a Denver area gay couple, last year.

But Jack Phillips, one of the owners, declined to make the cake citing his Christian beliefs.

"We would close down the bakery before we compromised our beliefs," he told KCNC, adding that protests and petitions will not make him change his mind.

We have Americans being threatened with jail time for doing nothing more than refusing to affirmatively sanction an event that goes against Christianity. In other words, liberals aren't just trying to make gay marriage legal; they're trying to make opposition to gay marriage illegal.

5) Air Force Veteran Faces A Court Martial For Opposing Gay Marriage: Under Barack Obama, the military has become aggressively anti-Christian and pro-gay to such an extent that the troops are no longer even allowed to privately oppose gay marriage.

Senior Master Sgt. Phillip Monk found himself at odds with his Lackland Air Force Base commander after he objected to her plans to severely punish an instructor who had expressed religious objections to homosexuality. During the conversation, his commander ordered him to share his personal views on homosexuality.

"I was relieved of my position because I don't agree with my commander's position on gay marriage," he told me. "We've been told that if you publicly say that homosexuality is wrong, you are in violation of Air Force policy."

...Last week, Monk was supposed to meet with an Air Force investigator tasked with gathering facts about the complaint. But when he arrived, Monk was immediately read his Miranda Rights and accused of providing false statements in a conversation Monk had with Fox's Todd Starnes.

After he was relieved of his duties, the Liberty Institute filed a religious discrimination complaint on his behalf. ..."I immediately got the sense that this was retaliation against me for coming forward with my religious discrimination complaint," he said.

The accusations against Monk are a court-martial offense in the Air Force – and it's quite possible that the 19-year veteran with a spotless record could be booted out of the military because of his Christian beliefs. And he's not the only Christian at Lackland Air Force Base facing persecution for opposing gay marriage, according to Monk's pastor.

If you think the military has problems recruiting soldiers now, let the military keep persecuting Christians for their faith and see how well it does over the long haul. Of course, that wouldn't upset the Left one bit, but the rest of us should be concerned.

6) Government Forces Churches To Get Permits For Baptisms: Nevertheless, the Park Service recently began a new policy requiring churches that wished to hold baptisms in public waters to apply for a special permit at least 48 hours in advance of the baptism. The Park Service justified this recent demand by saying that the permits were necessary to "maintain park natural/cultural resources and quality visitor experiences, specific terms and conditions have been established."

…On August 21, Rep. Jason Smith (Missouri, R) heeded the complaints of his constituents and wrote a letter to the NPS asking what the heck was going on…

Between citizen outrage and Rep. Smith's threat to bring the matter before the full Congress, however, the Park Service quickly reversed its new policy, writing to the Congressman that, "As of today, the park's policy has been clarified to state that no permit will be required for baptisms within the Riverways. I can assure you the National Park Service has no intention of limiting the number of baptisms performed within the park."

When the government demands that a church get a permit to do baptisms, it's also tacitly saying it has the right to deny that permit. That's not acceptable.

7) Florida Professor Demands Student Stomp On Jesus: It all started

with a conflict between an antagonistic professor and one brave student at Florida Atlantic University. Ryan Rotela was told by his professor to write Jesus Christ's name on a piece of paper and stomp on it. Rotela defiantly refused and in retaliation, a formal disciplinary action was started against him.

But, before the system could roll over Rotela, a funny thing happened. The word about what was happening to him got out, Christians became outraged, and suddenly the university's tune quickly changed. "FAU's Senior Vice President for Student Affairs, Dr. Charles Brown, has since issued a groveling formal apology." Next thing you know, the disciplinary action was waved off.

Now, comes word that the professor, Deandre Poole, has been put on administrative leave following a withering public response, that included complaints from the Governor of Florida, Rick Scott.

Unfortunately, that story didn't have a happy ending. Even after the governor got involved, Deandre Poole still kept his job. However, had Christians not risen up, the student who refused to stomp on Jesus would have been the one punished while the professor would have paid no price at all. Moreover, you can be sure there won't be any more Jesus stomping going on in the classrooms at Florida Atlantic University any time soon.

If there's a lesson here, it's that when Christians refuse to back down, we usually win. What that means is if enough Christians stand up for our faith, you'll be surprised how fast the people in power lose their nerve about going after us. End of article.

Theamericanthinker.com reports another article titled, 'Christianity Under Attack in America.' It was written by Janet Levy, October 25, 2013. It reads:

"According to information released at a May 9, 2013 press conference by the families of Navy SEALs killed in an August 2011 helicopter shoot-down in Afghanistan, "military brass prohibited any mention of a Judeo-Christian G-d" and "invited a Muslim cleric to the funeral for the fallen Navy SEAL Team VI heroes who disparaged in Arabic the memory of these servicemen by damning them as infidels to Allah."

The accusations arose over a "ramp ceremony" held at Bagram Airfield in Afghanistan as flag-draped caskets of the dead soldiers were loaded onto a plane for transport back to the United States. The shocking words of the Muslim cleric, revealed in later translations, were spoken at a memorial service meant to honor those who made the ultimate sacrifice for their country. They were yet another example of the abject disrespect of Christians and Christianity endemic to the Muslim world.

Here at home, Christianity and Christian religious practices are also under attack, but in more subtle ways and under a misinterpretation of the principle of freedom of religion. In the United States, that legal doctrine is cited to marginalize Christian prayer and traditions, while, at the same time, dramatically accommodating and even expanding Muslim religious practices. Myriad examples exist.

During the recent government shutdown, Catholic priests were warned that they could be arrested for celebrating Mass, even if performed on a voluntary basis. Under Secretary of Defense Chuck Hagel's direction and determination was that priests do not "contribute to the morale" and "well-being" of military personnel." Thus, offering of the sacraments was prohibited and the Eucharist placed under lock and key. Curiously, no mention was made of curtailing religious freedom for Muslim service members or furloughing imams.

This prohibition against Christian religious practice is not limited to the military. Police throughout the land also frequently come down hard against Christians. In 2010, a group of students from the Arizona-based Wickenburg Christian Academy were ordered by a police officer to cease their quiet prayers on the steps of the Supreme Court in Washington, D.C. The officer cited a statute that prohibits demonstrations on the steps, but no official policy bars prayer at that location.

In June of 2010, David Wood and two other Christian missionaries were arrested by Dearborn, Michigan, police at the annual Arab festival for discussing Christianity on a public sidewalk outside the event. The men, who have since been acquitted, were charged with disturbing the peace and spent the night in jail.

Contrast these incidents with a massive public display of praying Muslims during the annual Muslim Day Parade in New York City. Muslims, who are protected each year during the event by Muslim NYPD officers, are free to engage in mass prayer, even prostrating themselves on the streets of midtown Manhattan. Vehicular traffic halts and participants freely harass non-Muslims who attempt to pass through the area on foot.

Meanwhile, the ACLU has been at the forefront of an extensive effort to ban Christian prayer from public schools under the "separation of church and state" provision of the First Amendment. This is a signature issue for the "civil rights" organization. However, for Muslim prayers, the organization reverses its interpretation and fights for student rights to engage in prayer.

For example, when Carver Elementary School in San Diego instituted a 15-minute prayer period during class time for Muslim students in 2004, the ACLU endorsed the practice. ACLU spokesman Kevin Keenan said the group supported Muslim prayer under the First Amendment's prohibition against impeding religion. In this way, the ACLU was "honoring constitutional standards for freedom of religion."

Again in 2010, the ACLU mustered only mild to nonexistent concern when 6th-graders from a Wellesley, Massachusetts's middle school took a field trip to a local mosque at the Islamic Society of Boston Cultural Center and engaged in prayer. Parents were told that students would learn about the architecture of the building and observe a midday prayer service. But once at the mosque -- which is associated with the Muslim Brotherhood, known supporters of Islamic terrorism -- students were told by a mosque official that "Allah is the only G-d" and taught how to recite the midday prayer. After being encouraged to join the Muslim men, some of the boys prostrated themselves to Allah.

Meanwhile, in Michigan, Dearborn public schools have a policy of accommodating Muslim prayers at school during school hours, as well as ignoring unexcused absences for Muslims to leave school early for Friday prayers. Yet, in 2009, after a Muslim organization complained about permission slips given to Christian students to attend off-site after-school Bible study, issuance of the slips was discontinued.

In addition to police, the ACLU, and schools, U.S. courts have also sided with the Islamic religion and against Christianity. In 2001, the Byron Union School District in Byron, California instituted a three-week unit on Islam for 7th-graders. Students took Muslim names, recited Islamic prayers, and celebrated Ramadan. When parents sued the school on the grounds that the course was "officially endorsing a religion," the U.S. Supreme Court rejected their appeal, leaving intact an earlier ruling by the Ninth U.S. Circuit Court of Appeals that deemed that the unit did not violate the Constitution and had an "instructional purpose."

In 2009, the same court of appeals upheld a ban by Henry Jackson High School officials in Everett, Washington against an instrumental performance of Ave Maria at a 2006 commencement ceremony. A student futilely challenged the school's determination that the song was "an obvious religious piece" at a graduation that should be "strictly secular."

Government entities also bear down on the Christian religion. After allowing baptisms in Sinking Creek in the Ozarks for an almost uninterrupted 50-year span, the National Park Service in August notified Gladden Baptist Church in Salem, Missouri that permits would now be required in advance of baptism ceremonies in the waterway. The requirement was later rescinded in response to the intervention of local Congressman Jason Smith.

And this month, in Ovid, Colorado, the director of a city-owned cemetery initially refused to inscribe the Ichthus or "Jesus fish" on the tombstone of a local preacher's wife on the grounds that some people might be offended. Despite the fact that the cemetery is filled with headstones inscribed with religious symbols and Biblical verses, city officials refused to come to the family's aid. The cemetery director defended his position with a logic-defying hypothetical: "What if someone wanted to put a swastika?" -- thereby disrespectfully equating a representation of Christ with a symbol associated with Nazi Germany. The city reversed itself only after public outcry and media attention.

The instances listed above make it readily apparent that the First Amendment is often conveniently misinterpreted to buttress the assault on the Christian religion and its expression, practice, and traditions. In this way, Christianity is being insidiously expunged from public life using false legal pretenses. The legitimate interpretation of the provisions of the First Amendment, which include prohibitions against government interference in public religious expression and the establishment of a national religion, has been twisted to prohibit Christian prayer in public places and schools. This is a false reading of "separation of church and state."

Yet, as the instances listed above and many others illustrate, this interpretation doesn't apply to "mosque and state." Freedom of religion has come to mean no freedom for the practice of Christianity but ample freedom to practice Islam. If the war on Christianity in America isn't halted soon, Barack Obama's statement that "Whatever we once were, we are no longer a Christian nation," will certainly become a reality." End of article.

Air Force Removes Bible: By Todd Starnes, Foxnews.com, 31 March 2014. Below is the article:

On March 14 Air Force Chief of Staff Gen. Mark Welsh told members of the House Armed Services committee that there was no war on religious liberty.

"The single biggest frustration I've had in this job is the perception that somehow there is religious persecution inside the United States Air Force," the general told lawmakers. "It is not true."

"Rep. John Fleming (R-La.) told me the Air Force seems to be the worst offender when it comes to attacks on religious liberty.

If that's true, perhaps Gen. Welsh could explain why a Bible was removed from a POW/MIA Missing Man Table at Patrick Air Force Base in Florida. The removal of the Good Book was first reported by the Gannett-owned newspaper Florida Today.

Base officials confirmed to Fox News Monday that the entire Missing Man Table display had been removed from a dining hall because of the Bible. A press statement said the inclusion of the Bible ignited "controversy and division."

Missing Man Tables are a long honored military tradition. The tables serve as a reminder of the plight of brave Americans who are missing in action or who are being held prisoner of war. The display includes a white table cloth setting with an inverted glass, a plate with lemon and salt, a single rose, a candle and a Bible.

Each item is an integral part of the Missing Man Table & Honors

Ceremony, according to the National League of Families of American Prisoners and Missing in Southeast Asia.

The Bible represents the strength gained through faith in our country, founded as one nation under God, to sustain those lost from our midst," the official ceremony document states.

However, someone at Patrick Air Force Base objected to the Bible's placement on the table.

The following is the Air Force's explanation of what happened:

"The 45th Space Wing deeply desires to honor America's Prisoners of War (POW) and Missing in Action (MIA) personnel. Unfortunately, the Bible's presence or absence on the table at the Riverside Dining Facility ignited controversy and division, distracting from the table's primary purpose of honoring POWs/MIAs. Consequently, we temporarily replaced the table with the POW/MIA flag in an effort to show our continued support of these heroes while seeking an acceptable solution to the controversy. After consultation with several relevant organizations, we now intend to re-introduce the POW/MIA table in a manner inclusive of all POWs/MIAs as well as Americans everywhere."

The Air Force did not say when the Missing Man Table would be returned. Nor did they say whether the Bible would be included in the display. They also declined to explain what they meant by the word "inclusive."

Retired Lt. Gen. Jerry Boykin, now an executive vice president with the Family Research Council, denounced the Air Force Academy's actions.

"I'm still looking for somebody in a leadership position in the Air Force with an ounce of courage," he told me. "They buckle to an extreme minority group every time and constitutionally they are simply wrong."

Rep. John Fleming (R-La.) told me the Air Force seems to be the worst offender when it comes to attacks on religious liberty.

"It's very disconcerting that all it takes is for someone to be offended by that – and it comes down," he said. "The First Amendment is very clear on this. Speech may offend some people – in this case maybe Christianity offends some people in the Air Force – but that doesn't matter. We're still allowed to speak about our closely held beliefs."

Fleming accused the Air Force of ignoring the law.

"Since when does one unnamed, unknown individual have veto power over the First Amendment rights of all people in the military and in this case the Air Force?" he asked.

Ann Mills-Griffiths is the chairman of the National League of POW/MIA Families. She told me she was glad the Air Force base is going to reinstall the Missing Man Table, but she wonders if the new display will include the Bible.

She said the Bible is "part of the Missing Man Honor Ceremony and we hope it will be restored to what it was."

"Our country is one nation under God," she said. "It doesn't seem outrageous or unreasonable to have the Bible on the table."

Ron Crews, the executive director of the Chaplain Alliance for Religious Liberty, told me he hopes the Air Force will restore the Bible to its rightful place. He called it a symbol of hope and courage for military personnel and their families.

"It is sad when military traditions honoring our POWs and MIAs are trumped by pursuits to remove any vestige of the faith that has sustained our warriors since Valley Forge," Crews told me.

Earlier this month, a cadet at the Air Force Academy removed an inspirational Bible verse from a white board hanging outside his dorm room. Air Force officials said the cadet "voluntarily" removed the verse after someone complained.

However, Liberty Institute attorney Michael Berry said he was told by officials at the Air Force Academy that had the cadet not voluntarily removed the verse, he would have been ordered to remove it.

Berry told OneNewsNow.com the incident was a clear denial of the cadet's right of freedom of religious expression.

He said, "well, the Air Force's official policy – and this is coming from the very top, from the Pentagon level – is that the term 'free exercise of religion' does not extend to speech of this kind," Berry told the news organization. "Either verbal speech or writing a verse on a whiteboard, he said, would not fall under the protection of free exercise of religion as it is written in the First Amendment."

I would certainly be remiss if I did not extend my thanks to the staff of Florida Today, for first reporting this latest incident of religious liberty under attack.

General Welsh's remarks from March 14 bear repeating. He claimed there is no religious persecution happening in the Air Force. If that's the case, sir, what have you done with the Bible? End of article.

Todd Starnes is host of Fox News & Commentary, heard on hundreds of radio stations. His latest book is "God Less America."

Another article about the Air Force and Bibles. This article is by Thechristianexaminer.com:

The Air Force has removed Bibles from its list of items that are provided in on-base lodging facilities.

The Military Association of Atheists and Freethinkers filed a complaint when an atheist, stationed at Kadena Airbase in Japan, contacted them to find out why there was a Bible in the Air Force lodging.

The Air Force responded by removing the Bibles from Air Force hotels and from its checklist of items that are provided in approved lodging facilities.

According to a statement released by the National Prayer Caucus, "After receiving a complaint by the Military Association of Atheists and Freethinkers, the Air Force will remove 'Is a Bible provided?' from the checklist that staff at Air Force Inns use when ensuring that rooms comply with lodging standards."

Col. Ron Crews, executive director for the Chaplain Alliance expressed his concern over the decision by Air Force officials to remove Bibles from the checklist of items in on-base lodging rooms stating that it is creating a "religion free" zone in the Air Force.

"From General George Washington until today military personnel have taken counsel, received comfort, and been encouraged by biblical texts," said Crews. "These Bibles cost the Air Force nothing, and their presence is legally legitimate; therefore, no reason exists for the Air Force to have retreated in the face of the small anti-religious group that demanded removal of the books."

Air Force Services Agency spokesman Michael Dickerson has reportedly stated that the Air Force has "no requirement to have Bibles in the lodging checklist."

"While there is no requirement to have them, why should there be a requirement to remove them?" Col. Crews said. "They are provided free of charge as a service. No airman is required to pick one up or read it. The Bibles are merely there to use if desired. This pending decision is one more example of religious cleansing in the Air Force, and it must stop."

Crews also noted that other faith groups have also provided religious materials, such as the Koran.

An Air Force official said, "After a legal review, the Air Force Services Agency determined that there was no legal reason to have the question on the lodging checklist." Bibles are placed in Air Force Inn rooms by the Gideons, at no cost to the government. End of article.

Chick-fil-A Banned From Donating 200 Sandwiches to a School Fundraiser From: Thefederalistpapers.org:

'Chick-fil-A BANNED From Donating 200 Sandwiches to a School Fundraiser For The Most Ridiculous Reason,' By Steve Straub on September 12, 2014:

A Chick-fil-A restaurant in Ventura, California had offered to donate 200 meals worth $600 to the local high school for a fundraising event. In the past this Chick-fil-A location had donated thousands of dollars to the school.

This time around the school's principal banned Chik-fil-A from contributing sandwiches to the fund raiser because someone might get offended over the stance towards gay marriage held by the President of the company.

From Fox News:

Feathers have been ruffled at California's Ventura High School, where the principal this week banned the football booster club from selling Chick-fil-A sandwiches over fears that people might be offended.

What, pray tell, could people find offensive about a plump juicy chicken breast tucked between two buttered buns?

Were English teachers put off by the restaurant chain's grammatically challenged bovine pitchmen?

Did the waffle fries and banana pudding milkshakes exceed the nutritional limits deemed acceptable by the federal government?

The answer, dear readers, is no. It seems Principal Val Wyatt's ban has less to do with poultry and more to do with politics.

"With their political stance on gay rights and because the students of Ventura High School and their parents would be at the event, I didn't want them on campus," Wyatt told the Ventura County Star.

It was a sentiment supported by Trudy Tuttle Ariaga, superintendent of the Ventura Unified School District.

"We value inclusivity and diversity on our campus, and all our events and activities are going to adhere to our mission," Ariaga told CBS News in Los Angeles.

Remember when Chick-fil-A told their customers that gay people were not welcome at their stores? Me neither.

The local Chick-fil-A franchise has a storied history of supporting the school district – to the tune of thousands of dollars – and owner Robert Shaffer had generously offered to give the booster club 200 meals for a "back-to-school" event on Wednesday at which they expected to raise $1,600 for the football team, the Ventura Star reported.

"That would have gone toward the football program, everything from uniforms to food for the boys," booster club president Dan Swim told the Star. "We don't charge money for the boys to play football."

"Chick-fil-A doesn't have a stance on gay marriage," Shaffer told the Star. "We treat everyone who walks through our doors, regardless of their religion or sexual orientation, with honor, dignity and respect."

Helmet Cross Decal Banned From Arkansas State University Football Team. From: Religion News Service By Dan Wolken Posted: 09/12/2014 10:40 am EDT Updated: 09/12/2014 10:59 am EDT: KAIT-Jonesboro, AR-News, weather, sports.

(RNS) Arkansas State is removing a Christian cross decal from the back of its football helmets after a complaint that it violated separation of church and state, the university said Wednesday (Sept. 10).

Athletics director Terry Mohajir said he wanted to fight the decision because the decal was intended to honor former player Markel Owens and equipment manager Barry Weyer, who both died this year. However, Mohajir said he had little choice but to follow advice from the university's legal counsel to remove or modify the symbol.

"My job is to support our players and our coaches in their expression of any type of grief, and that's what I was doing," Mohajir said.

Rebecca Markert, an attorney for the Freedom From Religion Foundation, said her organization had been looking into the matter since hearing about the decals over the weekend but had not yet lodged a formal complaint with Arkansas State.

"That is great news," Markert said of the school's decision. "Putting religious imagery on public school property is unconstitutional."

The Freedom From Religion Foundation has been looking into potential church-state separation issues at college football programs during the past year, particularly at Clemson and Ole Miss. Markert said the organization recently filed an open records request with Ole Miss regarding its chaplain program.

According to documents provided to USA Today by Arkansas State, Jonesboro, Ark., attorney Louis Nisenbaum sent an email to University Counsel Lucinda McDaniel on Saturday, pointing out that he noticed the crosses while watching Arkansas State's game at Tennessee earlier that day.

"That is a clear violation of the Establishment Clause as a state endorsement of the Christian religion," Nisenbaum wrote. "Please advise whether you agree and whether ASU will continue this practice."

On Monday, McDaniel emailed Mohajir, saying she found no specific legal cases that addressed crosses on football helmets but recommending that the bottom of the cross could be cut off so the symbol would be a plus sign.

"While we could argue that the cross with the initials of the fallen student and trainer merely memorialize their passing, the symbol we have authorized to convey that message is a Christian cross," she wrote. "Persons viewing the helmets will, and have, seen the symbol as a cross and interpreted that symbol as an endorsement of the Christian religion. This violates the legal prohibition of endorsing religion."

Mohajir said the original idea for the decal came from a leadership committee of players and that wearing it was voluntary.

"Any time our players have an expression of faith and wanting to honor two members of the football program, I'm 100 percent behind them," he said. End of article.

A nation accepting ungodly acts is also defiled. From: biblehub.com/revelation.

"Leviticus 18 lists many acts of nakedness and sexual activity such as adultery and incest not tolerated by God. Verses 22 and 23 specifically identify homosexuality as an abomination, and bestiality as confusion. However as Leviticus pertains to America, and other countries, verses 24 through 28 are most applicable. In summary, those verses state that if a nation accepts these ungodly actions by its individuals then that nation is also defiled: "therefore I do visit the iniquity thereof upon it, and the land itself vomiteth out her inhabitants." 27: "For all these abominations have the men of the land done, which were before you, and the land it defiled." 28: That the land spue not you out also, when ye defile it, as it spued out the nations that were before you."

Perhaps this next article gives an example of this idea. It's from Godfatherpolitics.com. and was submitted by Dave Jolly in September, 2013. The article begins:

"Gay activists are successfully getting laws passed in cities around the country that discriminate against Christians. The laws are called nondiscrimination laws by the LGBT activists pushing through one city council after another. So far, over 180 cities have passed these so-called nondiscrimination ordinances.

In essence the laws provide special protection to LGBT individuals while at the same time; they place huge restrictions on the religious rights of Christians. For instance, the San Antonio city council voted 8-3 to pass their ordinance that bans any form of discrimination based upon sexual orientation or gender identity. Their ban went so far as to forbid anyone who does not openly accept or support gay rights from conducting any business with the city. Violating the ordinance is a Class C misdemeanor that could result in a fine of up to $500 per day.

If a pastor is preaching on Sunday and says anything about homosexuality being a sin in the eyes of God, he could be arrested for violating the ordinance. If you are in a private conversation with someone and say that you believe homosexuality is a sin or that you are uncomfortable around someone because they are gay, you could be arrested. The way LGBT activists operate these days, I can see them visiting churches just to try to catch the pastor or someone else saying anything against homosexuality just so they can run to the city to have them arrested.

This is the concern of many Christian leaders throughout San Antonio and other cities that have passed similar laws. Jacob Herrera with Faith Outreach International commented, saying:

"The right for us to speak out and say, 'I disagree. It doesn't sound right.' Now we're labeled a hater, a bigot, homophobic."

Rosalie Astran, a member of Abundant Life Church reacted to San Antonio's ordinance saying:

"My faith, my belief and how I've raised my family—I can get in trouble for that because they don't agree with that."

Carleton Soules, San Antonio Councilman who voted no on the ordinance was deeply concerned about how the ordinance was rushed thru the system. He stated:

"We didn't put the ordinance up on the website. It was fast-tracked through. Anytime we are going at light speed to do something that's unpopular that throws a lot of red flags."

"I believe if you're a small business owner, operating within the city limits of San Antonio, or you're a business owner that wants to do business with the city, you need to tread carefully."

These non (or anti) discrimination ordinances echo the hate language measures that the United Nations has been trying to push on everyone. One thing they all have in common is that it is illegal to discriminate against anyone for race, gender, gender identification, sexual orientation and religion, provided you're not a Christian. It's perfectly legal and allowable to discriminate against Christians and restrict their rights of religion and free speech.

We seem to be the only demographic group that can be slandered, insulted, urinated on, and told what we are and are not allowed to say. In some areas like California, homosexuals can counsel and provide therapy for those confused about their sexual orientation, but

Christians are not legally allowed to provide the same counseling and therapy to the same confused individuals.

Today, we find nearly 200 cities with nondiscriminatory ordinances. By the end of the year the number will most likely be well over 200. It wouldn't surprise me to see a federal law passed sometime before the end of 2014 that discriminates against Christians and provides the special protection for gays. If left unchecked, by the end of 2015 we could well see any public show of Christianity to be outlawed because it offends someone somewhere. No one cares about offending Christians because we're just lower class citizens anyway." End of Article.

Jindal: Religious war against Christians in US: By The Associated Press 9:37 p.m. CDT May 10, 2014:

Elitist intellectuals and liberals are waging a religious war against Christians, trying to silence them, Louisiana Gov. Bobby Jindal told graduates of Liberty University on Saturday.

"The new left in America is completely intolerant of people of faith," Jindal said. "The left no longer wants to debate. They simply want to silence us."

Jindal said abundant evidence includes the experiences of the Benham brothers and Phil Robertson of "Duck Dynasty."

HGTV canceled "Flip it Forward" — a real estate show featuring brothers David and Jason Benham — before a scheduled October debut after the lobbying group Right Wing Watch labeled David

Benham an "anti-gay extremist" and reported on statements he made against homosexuality and gay marriage.

The A&E network briefly suspended "Duck Dynasty" patriarch Phil Robertson after GQ magazine quoted him as saying that homosexuals are sinners and that African Americans were happy under Jim Crow laws establishing segregation.

"They have the right to speak their minds, no matter how indelicately they choose to do so," Jindal said Saturday. "The war of religious liberty is the war of free speech."

Jindal and university president Jerry Falwell Jr. spoke during a ceremony that took nearly two hours.

The university said nearly 17,500 students were graduated from its residential and online programs, with more than 6,000 of them among the 35,000 people at Williams Stadium in Lynchburg.

Jindal said much of American culture has become secular, but religious freedom invented America and faith sustains it.

He urged the graduates to stand up for their Christian education and their beliefs.

"If God is with us, then who can be against us?" he said. End of article.

Now, these actions against American Christians concern only ideology and belief. The next chapter demonstrates how far it could go.

Chapter 7

War Everywhere

While the war against Christians in the Western world is insidious and just now moving into a harsher environment, other parts of the world present examples of just how harsh and dogmatic this war can become. In many other parts of the world the consequences of the war's harshness result in death - death without any hesitation or remorse. That harshness and inhuman treatment is guided by a 'strange god' worshiped by many in those more dogmatic environments - toward which America is leaning. What is that strange god and where did he come from?

In one of his early speeches, Obama said, "We are no longer a Christian nation - not just." Obviously he recognizes other 'religions,' one of which is Islam. How much longer will he be able to hide his support for that 'strange god?'

When the numbers are large enough will he transition the United

States from what was a Christian nation into a Muslim nation or that godless nation of the strange god. Daniel, Chapter 11, Verses 38 and 39 introduces that strange god:

38: "But in his estate shall he honour the God of forces: and a god whom his fathers knew not shall he honour with gold, and silver, and with precious stones, and pleasant things."

39: "Thus shall he do in the most strong holds with a strange god, whom he shall acknowledge and increase with glory: and he shall cause them to rule over many, and shall divide the land for gain."

Daniel wrote this 500 years before Christ was born. Muslims didn't discover their god until 600 years after Christ was born. When Daniel wrote this, any god unknown at his time would be a strange god would it not? The Islamists' god is the only one unknown when Daniel wrote this information.

Another interesting point: many basics of Islamic beliefs seem to be carbon copies directly from the Christian religion. For example: their antichrist is named - Dajjal. Their savior-messiah is named - Mahdi. The Sunnis and Shites hate each other mainly because of their disagreement about the arrival of their Mahdi. (Another interesting question: who has divided our land for gain? America is no longer one nation under God with liberty and justice for all. Who has driven the stake between the hearts of Americans with his call for 'fair share' and 'redistribute the wealth?')

Strange isn't it that their god is different, but all the information surrounding their god seems very similar to historical events 600 years preceding that discovery. Regardless of the source of their god, that god's name is used by his most extreme followers as justification to slaughter many innocents in the darker nations. African Christians now suffer greatly in that strange god's name

The following is an article from LAGOS (AFP) reported by Aderogba Obisesan on September 7, 2014. The heading is, "Christians in northeast Nigeria are paying a heavy price at the hands of Boko Haram, even if they are not being targeted specifically by the militants in their bloody quest for an Islamic state."

Several towns in the northeastern states of Yobe, Borno and Adamawa have been attacked in recent weeks, sending thousands of residents fleeing and raising concerns about the speed of the Islamists' deadly rampage.

Madagali in Adamawa has a large number of Christians and was overrun last week. The Islamists also seized Gulak, the headquarters of Madagali local government council, this weekend.

The Islamists vandalized and destroyed churches and church buildings and singled out Christians who remained, according to residents.

"Christians in the town are really in a terrible situation, a moment of great persecution," said Father Gideon Obasogie, the spokesman for the Roman Catholic Diocese of Maiduguri, which stretches from Yobe, through Borno to Adamawa.

"Christian men were caught and beheaded, the women were forced to become Muslim and were taken as wives to the terrorists."

"Some Boko Haram sympathizers around the town identified Christian homes to be occupied and the Christians hiding were also identified and killed. Strict Sharia law had been promulgated."

Schools, Christian churches and religious buildings have been repeatedly attacked and razed during the five-year insurgency.A declaration by Boko Haram leader Abubakar Shekau in a video released last month that the captured Borno town of Gwoza was now part of an Islamic caliphate has only heightened Christian fears of persecution.

But the Bishop of Maiduguri, Oliver Dashe, told AFP: "Both Christians and Muslims are always killed because a bomb blast does not discriminate between who is a Christian or a Muslim.

"However, from the waves of recent attacks, you could clearly say that the Christians are worst hit," he said in an email interview. Figures compiled by the diocese based on the testimony of residents and parishioners who have fled make for sober reading. Bishop Oliver said that more than 90,000 Catholics had been displaced in the recent fighting.

Between 2009 when the insurgency began and this year, more than 500 Catholics have been killed, 50 churches destroyed and three schools, including a seminary, razed. Nine other church schools have been shut. According to the United Nations, at least 650,000 people have fled their homes in recent years because of Boko Haram violence, fear of attack but also the often indiscriminate and violent reprisals by security forces.

Since 2009, the insurgency in Africa's most populous nation has claimed at least 10,000 lives according to the authorities but the true figure is impossible to verify independently.

"The situation for now seems out of control," said Bishop Dashe. "The terrorists should embrace dialogue and drop their arms."

Nigeria specialist Marc-Antoine Perouse de Montclos, said the Boko Haram insurgency is not an "inter-religious" conflict pitting Muslims against Christians.

"It's mainly a war between Muslims, an insurrection of Islamists against those who they consider bad Muslims," said Perouse de Montclos, from the French Institute of Geopolitics in Paris.

"Boko Haram has existed for about 15 years and they have attacked Christians but the majority of the victims are Muslims."

The heavily-armed group has previously attacked senior Muslim figures for recognizing and working with the constitutionally secular Nigerian government.

In Gamboru Ngala, a border town in Borno's far northeast which was overrun last week, the Islamists executed the town's most senior Muslim cleric, residents said.

The Emir of Gwoza was also killed in May during an attack on his convoy. Two other traditional rulers were attacked but escaped unharmed.

Boko Haram has even tried to assassinate two of the most senior and influential Muslim figures in Nigeria: the late emir of Kano and the Shehu of Borno, the number two and three Muslim leaders in the country. The most senior figure, the Sultan of Sokoto, has also been threatened.

"Boko Haram's agenda has not changed since its beginnings in 2002," said Perouse de Montclos." End of article.

Another article by Leonardo Blair, reporter at christianpost.com, May 16, 2014 gives more information in his article titled, 'Boko Haram in Nigeria:

"Abubakar Shekau, leader of the Islamic militant group Boko Haram, has made it clear that the recent abduction of nearly 300 mostly Christian schoolgirls in Nigeria is not merely about denying education to women but a war against the damaging effects of Christians and Christianity in Nigeria.

In a translation of a nearly 1-hour video by Sahara Reporters, he explained how wars were waged against countries like Iraq and Afghanistan in the name of Christianity and now there is a plan in motion to do the same in Nigeria.

"Here is what Bush once said and we will repeat it here. He said all the fights going on in Iraq and Afghanistan are Christian war, crusade, it is a known issue. And that they will crush Afghanistan, today I will say my own," said Shekau.

"To the people of the world, everybody should know his status, it is either you are with us Mujahedeen or you are with the Christians. The likes of Obama, Lincoln, Clinton, Jonathan, Aminu Kano. They are your fathers of democracy, the likes of Tafawa Balewa. It is Usman Dan Fodiyo that is our own," he continued.

"We know what is happening in this world, it is a Jihad war against Christians and Christianity. It is a war against western education, democracy and constitution," he said.

Shekau said despite the international outcry over the abduction of Nigerian schoolgirls, the Jihad hasn't even started in Nigeria yet.

"We have not started, next time we are going inside Abuja; we are going to refinery and town of Christians. Do you know me? I have no problem with Jonathan. This is what I know in Quran. This is a war against Christians and democracy and their constitution, Allah says we should finish them when we get them," he said.

He said Nigerian politicians consorting with western leaders in the name of progress and development is apostasy.

"You are sitting down in the name of clerics with turbans; you are sitting with Christians thinking it is mediation. Saying it is development and progress, what progress after you have deviated from Allah? We will die killing and slaughtering them, if you meet infidels in battle field brethren, just harvest their necks; Allah said it and not Shekau," he noted. He then ripped into human rights groups for promoting homosexuality.

"And you are saying you are advocates of human rights. Humor sexual people like you, promoters of same sex marriage, animals knows rights more than them, even sheep doesn't sleep with sheep, but you keep a woman and a woman as husband and wife," he said. End of Article.

The War on The Remnant of Her Seed

This is an article by Paul Marshall, CP Op-Ed Contributor, published on June 16, 2014. It describes the widespread war on 'the remnant of her seed.' Current-day Christians certainly are remnants of the seed of Christianity's beginning.

"For at least three reasons, the contemporary persecution of Christians demands attention: It is occurring on a massive scale, it is under reported, and in many parts of the world it is rapidly growing.

The Pew Forum on Religion and Public Life finds that Christians are suffering persecution in more places today than any other religious group; between 2006 and 2012, Pew says, they were targeted for harassment in 151 countries-three-quarters of the world's states. Similar findings are reported by the Vatican, Newsweek, the Economist, and the 60-year-old Christian support group Open Doors. Most people in the West are unaware of these facts, though that may be changing.

A few cases do get press coverage-the desperate plight of Meriam Ibrahim, for instance, who gave birth in a Sudanese prison just the other day. She was raised a Christian, but after officials learned that her long-absent father was a Muslim; she was sentenced to death for apostasy-for leaving Islam. And since in Sudan a Muslim woman may not be married to a Christian, her marriage to her American husband was declared void, and she was convicted of adultery and sentenced to 100 lashes to be administered before her execution. These punishments will be dropped if she renounces her Christian faith, which she steadfastly refuses to do.

And, most notorious, the abduction into slavery of hundreds of schoolgirls in Nigeria on April 14 by the al Qaeda-linked Boko Haram led news cycles and tweets for a time, though the religious dimensions of the story were often played down. While the kidnapped girls include Muslims (Boko Haram regards them as apostates because of their Western education), most are Christians, seized in a predominantly Christian area and now subjected to forced conversion.

These events get media attention because they are particularly poignant, or dramatic, or involve foreigners, but our media miss countless other stories. Since the kidnappings, Boko Haram has killed-not kidnaped, killed-hundreds of people, many in the predominantly Christian Gwoza area of Borno State, destroyed 36 churches, and kidnapped at least 8 more girls. On June 1, it attacked a Christian area in neighboring Adamawa state, killing 48 people.

In Sudan, a second woman, Faiza Abdalla, has been arrested on suspicion of converting to Christianity, and on April 8 a court terminated her marriage to a Catholic. Iran is imprisoning and torturing pastors from the rapidly growing house church movement, including an American citizen, Pastor Saeed Abedini.

Another case receiving attention is North Korea's sentencing of a South Korean missionary, Kim Jong-uk, to life with hard labor. On May 30, he was convicted of espionage and trying to start a church.

North Korea also still holds Kenneth Bae, an American sentenced to 15 years' hard labor on charges of trying to use religion to overthrow the political system.

The Chinese government's demolition of the 3,000-member Sanjiang church in Wenzhou on April 28 was newsworthy partly because of the church's size, but also because Sanjiang was not an "underground" church but an official, approved, government-registered "Three-Self" church. Some 20 other official churches in the area have had all or parts of their buildings removed or demolished, and hundreds more are threatened with destruction.

Vietnam has imprisoned over 60 Christian leaders. Eritrea holds more than 1,000 Christians in conditions so inhumane that prisoner's die or are permanently crippled. In Somalia, in an ignored religious genocide, Al-Shabaab systematically hunts Christians and kills those it finds.

Of course, people of all religions suffer persecution for their faith or lack thereof-the situations of Baha'is and Jews in Iran, Ahmadis and Hindus in Pakistan, Tibetan Buddhists and Falun Gong in China, independent Buddhists in Vietnam, and Rohingya Muslims in Burma are particularly dire. Traditionally, the United States has been regarded as the country that advocates religious freedom for all, often to the disdain of other Westerners. In recent years, however, that has changed. Now America is quieter, while others speak up.

British prime minister David Cameron said recently that "our religion is now the most persecuted religion around the world" and "We should stand up against persecution of Christians and other religious groups wherever and whenever we can, and should be unashamed in doing so." German chancellor Angela Merkel has repeatedly stressed that Christians are the world's most widely persecuted religious group. Probably most outspoken of all is Vladimir Putin; no doubt this reflects geopolitical calculation, but the fact remains that he is stressing the matter.

The Italian Foreign Ministry has established an "Observatory on Religious Freedom." Quite properly, it is concerned with all religions, but its genesis was the upsurge in killings of Christians. Two years ago it hosted a conference on "Stopping the Massacre of Christians in Nigeria." Former French foreign minister Bernard Kouchner established a similar agency in the Quai d'Orsay, and later the ministry gave financial backing to an "Observatory of Cultural and Religious Pluralism" devoted to monitoring "attacks on freedom of conscience, on freedom of expression, and freedom of religion around the world," particularly with respect to the Arab Spring. Canada now has an ambassador-at-large for religious freedom, a title borrowed from the United States.

In the United States, meanwhile, the position of U.S. ambassador-at-large for religious freedom is vacant, as it has been for over half of President Barack Obama's tenure. Even when the position has been filled, in the last decade it has usually been marginalized. President Obama gave a great speech on religious freedom at the National Prayer Breakfast, but little action followed. The United States has marginalized the issue in other ways, too.

After the massacre of 25 Copts by the Egyptian military on October 9, 2011, the White House lamented the "tragic loss of life among demonstrators and security forces" (emphasis added) and called for "restraint on all sides." As my colleague Sam Tadros commented, "I call upon the security forces to refrain from killing Christians, and upon Christians to refrain from dying."

On Easter morning in 2012, a church in Kaduna, Nigeria, was the target of a Boko Haram suicide car bombing that killed 39 and wounded dozens. (The previous Christmas, Boko Haram had bombed St. Theresa's Catholic Church outside the capital, Abuja, killing 44 worshipers, and also attacked churches in the towns of Jos, Kano, Gadaka, and Damaturu.) There was no official comment from the Obama administration about the Kaduna massacre on Christians' holiest day. Instead, Secretary of State Hillary Clinton issued a press release celebrating the Romani people and demanding that Europe become more inclusive of them.

At the beginning of the State Department's annual report on international religious freedom for 2013, Secretary of State John Kerry stated, "While Christians were a leading target of societal discrimination, abuse, and violence in some parts of the world, members of other religions, particularly Muslims, suffered as well." The assertion is incontrovertible, yet the wording elides the truth: Christians are not just "a leading target," they are the leading target. American officials seem so scared of being accused of selectively defending Christians that they consistently overcompensate and minimize what is happening.

The Catholic and Orthodox churches are more outspoken now than they were in the past, partly because the plight of their brethren, especially in the Middle East, is so stark. Pope Benedict XVI raised the issue many times. Pope Francis, speaking three days after the

September 22, 2013, suicide bombing of All Saints Church in Peshawar, Pakistan, in which over 80 congregants were killed, urged Christians to examine their consciences about their response to anti-Christian persecution: "Am I indifferent to that, or does it affect me like it's a member of the family? Does it touch my heart, or doesn't it really affect me, [to know that] so many brothers and sisters in the family are giving their lives for Jesus Christ?"

Cardinal Timothy Dolan, in his November 11, 2013, address as he stepped down from chairing the U.S. Conference of Catholic Bishops, spoke of the "Via Crucis currently being walked by so many of our Christian brothers and sisters in other parts of the world, who are experiencing lethal persecution on a scale that defies belief."

Ecumenical Patriarch Bartholomew I of Constantinople has observed that "even the simple admission of Christian identity places the very existence of [the] faithful in daily threat," and Metropolitan Hilarion, chairman of the Russian Orthodox Church's Department for External Church Relations, has been raising the issue with American churches for several years.

Happily, there are signs that some Americans are again paying attention to the issue. Last month on Capitol Hill, a wide coalition of Christian leaders was convened by the co-chairs of the Religious Minorities in the Middle East Caucus, representatives Frank Wolf of Virginia, a Republican, and Anna Eshoo of California, a Democrat. They committed themselves to a "Pledge of Solidarity and Call to Action for Religious Freedom in the Middle East."

Although the persecution of Christians is widespread, Nigeria is where most are actually being killed, North Korea is the most repressive, China represses the largest number, the Pledge of Solidarity focuses on the Middle East and specifically on Syria, Iraq, and Egypt. These are countries where the situation has deteriorated rapidly to the point where Christian communities-along with smaller religious minorities such as Mandeans, Yezidis, Baha'is, and Ahmadis-now face "an existential threat to their presence in the lands where Christianity has its roots."

In the last decade, half of Iraq's Christians have fled the country, and many others have fled to the Kurdish region. In three days last August, Egypt's Coptic Christians experienced the worst single attack against their churches in 700 years, with 40 churches utterly destroyed and over 100 other sites severely damaged. Tens of thousands of Copts are estimated to have fled their homeland. Syria's Christians, like all Syrians, are caught in the middle of a brutal war, but, according to the pledge, they "are also victims of beheadings, summary executions, kidnapings, and forcible conversions, in deliberate efforts to suppress or eradicate their religious faith."

Too often these communities in the ancient heartland of Christianity have been forgotten. Speaking in Rome in December, Baghdad's Catholic Chaldean patriarch, Louis Sako, lamented, "We feel forgotten and isolated. We sometimes wonder, if they kill us all, what would be the reaction of Christians in the West? Would they do something then?"

In Washington, pledges like this new one tend to have about as much staying power as campaign promises. Still, there are reasons to believe that the Pledge of Solidarity will have an effect.

For one thing, the breadth of the coalition behind it is remarkable. Speakers included Cardinal Donald Wuerl, archbishop of Washington, Archbishop Oshagan Choloyan of the Armenian Apostolic Church of America, Leith Anderson, president of the National Association of Evangelicals, and Greek Orthodox Metropolitan Methodios of Boston. Pledge signers include Southern Baptist Ethics & Religious Liberty Commission president Russell D. Moore, Sojourners' Jim Wallis, Episcopal Church presiding bishop Katharine Jefferts Schori, Anglican Church in North America archbishop Robert Duncan, Samaritan's Purse president Franklin Graham, Robert George of Princeton University, chair of the U.S. Commission on International Religious Freedom, and George Marlin, chair of Aid to the Church in Need-USA.

Also promising is the fact that the Pledge of Solidarity sets forth focused goals-the appointment of a special envoy on Middle East religious minorities (legislation to create this position has passed the House but is stalled in the Senate, reportedly by a hold placed by Republican Tom Coburn of Oklahoma), a review of foreign aid to ensure it upholds principles of religious freedom, and an effort to see that refugee and reconstruction assistance reaches all religious communities.

But the pledge will have its greatest effect if, rather than falling on deaf ears, it awakens rank-and-file Americans and others to the religious diversity of the Middle East and the plight of Christians there and elsewhere. When Pope Francis and Ecumenical Patriarch Bartholomew I met in Jerusalem in May, their joint communiqué echoed the pledge, singling out "the Churches in Egypt, Syria, and Iraq, which have suffered most grievously due to recent events." The concern expressed by these religious leaders and a handful of politicians is abundantly justified. Still missing is any large-scale mobilization of free people on behalf of persecuted Christians around the world." End of article.

Chapter 8

War in the Middle East

The war against Christians in the Middle East has existed for many years. Basically, it has become part of the established and accepted culture, and anyone visiting most of those countries must adhere to those extreme Muslim rules or they will be not only ostracized, they could even be beheaded for a simple freedom taken for granted in the United States - at least for the time being.

But what might happen in the future in our great 'Land of the free, and home of the brave?' Perhaps this next article by Michael Snyder at Infowars.com, December 10, 2013 might give a clue. It's titled, 'The American Dream:'

The "coming persecution of Christians" has already begun. It is already here. So why is the mainstream media in the United States almost totally silent about this phenomenon? When some politician somewhere around the globe inadvertently offends homosexuals or Muslims, it instantly makes headline news.

But very few Americans are even aware that it has been estimated that 100 million Christians are currently facing persecution and that approximately 100,000 Christians die for their faith each year. As you are about to see, Christians all over the world are being burned alive, beheaded, crucified, tortured to death and imprisoned in metal shipping containers just because of what they believe. This persecution goes on year after year and it is steadily intensifying. But the governments of the western world and the mainstream media are almost entirely ignoring what is happening.

The information shared below is extremely graphic. Some of the websites that normally run my articles may want to think twice before posting this one. The reason why I have included such graphic information is because I believe that it is very important to accurately communicate what is truly going on out there. People need to know the reality of the holocaust that is happening. The following are short excerpts from news stories about incidents of Christian persecution that took place in 12 different countries around the planet. Sadly, the vast majority of Americans have never even heard about any of these stories:

#1 Christian Taxi Driver Pulled Out Of His Cab And Beheaded In Egypt: One attack involved taxi driver Rafaat Aziz Mina, who was slaughtered in an Alexandria street just because he was Christian. In his early twenties, he was killed on 16 August by a mob of Islamists who took to the streets after news reached them about the military's action against their camps in Cairo.

An amateur video shot by a resident shows a mob blocking cars, checking the passengers inside. When Aziz's taxi was stopped, one of the protesters noted a cross hanging from the rear view mirror. Quickly, the young man was dragged out and kicked, punched and beaten to death. For several minutes, the extremists defiled the lifeless body kicking and spitting on it, concluding their performance by cutting off his head, which they left on the sidewalk.

#2 Tortured To Death By U.S.-Backed Al-Qaeda Rebels In Syria: In late October, the U.S-supported "opposition" invaded and occupied Sadad for over a week, till ousted by the nation's military. Among other atrocities, 45 Christians—including women and children—were killed, several tortured to death; Sadad's 14 churches, some ancient, were ransacked and destroyed; the bodies of six people from one family, ranging from ages 16 to 90, were found at the bottom of a well (an increasingly common fate for "subhuman" Christians).

#3 "Slaughtering Us Like Chickens" In The Central African Republic: Thousands of Christian civilians sought refuge at an airport guarded by French soldiers Friday, fleeing from the mostly Muslim ex-rebels with machetes and guns who rule the country a day after the worst violence to hit the chaotic capital in nine months.

When several French helicopters landed at the airport, people sang with joy as they banged on plastic buckets and waved rags into the air in celebration.

Outside the barbed wire fences of the airport, bodies lay decomposing along the roads in a capital too dangerous for many to collect the corpses. Thursday's clashes left at least 280 dead, according to national radio, and have raised fears that waves of retaliatory attacks could soon follow.

"They are slaughtering us like chickens," said Appolinaire Donoboy, a Christian whose family remained in hiding.

#4 Shot For Refusing To Convert To Islam In Libya: A group of Muslims robbed two Egyptian Christians living in Libya, then tied up and shot them to death after the two Copts refused their demand to convert to Islam, relatives said.

On a rural road in Derna District in northeastern Libya on Wednesday (Sept. 25), a group of Muslims surrounded Waleed Saad Shaker, 25, and Nash'at Shenouda Ishaq, 27, demanded their belongings and started beating them. During the strong-arm robbery, the relatives said, the Muslims demanded that Shaker and Ishaq recite the shahada, the declaration of conversion to Islam. When the two Orthodox Coptic Christians refused, the group of Muslims tied them up and shot them.

#5 Head Cut Off In Front Of A Camera For Converting To Christianity In Tunisia: A young man appears held down by masked men. His head is pulled back, with a knife to his throat. He does not struggle and appears resigned to his fate. Speaking in Arabic, the background speaker, or "narrator," chants a number of Muslim prayers and supplications, mostly condemning Christianity, which, because of the Trinity, is referred to as a polytheistic faith: "Let Allah be avenged on the polytheist apostate"; "Allah empower your religion, make it victorious against the polytheists"; "Allah, defeat the infidels at the hands of the Muslims," and "There is no god but Allah and Muhammad is his messenger."

Then, to cries of "Allahu Akbar!"— Allah is greater!"—the masked man holding the knife to the apostate's throat begins to slice away, severing the head completely after approximately one minute of graphic knife-carving, as the victim drowns in blood. Finally, the severed head is held aloft to more Islamic slogans of victory.

#6 50 Christians Burned To Death In Their Pastor's Home In Nigeria: Fifty members of a northern Nigerian church were burned to death in their pastor's house.

The attack by armed gunmen was only the first in a 12-village spree of violence that left over 100 dead in northern Nigeria's Plateau State, a region that had previously been outside Islamic terrorist group Boko Haram's operational area and is the largely Muslim Fulani tribesmen's homeland.

Yet Boko Haram claimed responsibility for the attacks and threatened even more violence.

#7 Two Brothers Crucified For Their Faith In Ivory Coast: Two peasant brothers were brutally crucified on "the example of Christ" as forces loyal to Ivory Coast President Alassane Ouattara continue to target perceived supporters of his ousted Christian predecessor, Laurent Gbagbo.

Raphael Aka Kouame died of his injuries; incredibly his younger brother, Kouassi Privat Kacou, survived the ordeal. The pair were badly beaten and tortured before being crudely nailed to cross-shaped planks by their hands and feet with steel spikes on 29 May.

#8 Angry Mob Of About 1,000 People Destroys A Church And Beats Christians In India: Shouting religious slogans, a mob estimated at

1,000 people has destroyed a Christian church under construction in northern India, according to a report received from church leaders in the region. The attack occurred Sunday.

With the building demolished, the mob began to beat the pastor, his mother and church members, who were able to flee and went into hiding for the night. The extent of their injuries is not known.

#9 Suicide Bombers Kill 81 At A Church In Pakistan: A pair of suicide bombers killed 81 people outside a church in northwestern Pakistan on Sunday in the deadliest attack yet on the country's Christian minority, reviving fears that the newly installed government is powerless to stop the resurgent Taliban's reign of terror.

The attack on the 19th-century All Saints Church in Peshawar took place as hundreds of worshipers were streaming out of the church, police chief Mohammad Ali Babakhel told the newspaper Dawn.

"The suicide bomber tried to attack the people, but when he was stopped by the police, he detonated the bomb," he said. "The second blast was carried out inside the church."

#10 80 Lashes For Drinking Communion Wine In Iran: An Iranian court sentenced four Iranian men to 80 whiplashes for drinking wine during communion and possession of a satellite antenna.

The court issued the sentence in the city of Rasht on October 6. Christian Solidarity Worldwide, an advocacy organization for religious freedom, reported on the punishment last week on its website.

#11 Imprisoned In Metal Shipping Containers In Eritrea: A representative of Open Doors, a charity that works with Christians under pressure for their faith, said that many Christian men and women are being held in underground dungeons, metal shipping containers and military detention centers.

"They face exposure, hard labor and insufficient food, water and hygiene. They are regularly denied medical treatment for malaria and pneumonia contracted while in prison or diseases like diabetes, hypertension or cancer that they may have arrived with," said the representative.

#12 Publicly Executed For Owning A Bible In North Korea: Eight people — their heads covered with white bags — were tied to stakes at a local stadium in the city of Wonsan, before authorities shot them with a machine gun, according to the source.

Wonsan authorities gathered a crowd of 10,000 people, including children, at Shinpoong Stadium and forced them to watch the killings. End of article.

This nytimes.com article by Kareem Fahim, August 20, 2013 gives more exaples:

NAZLA, Egypt — The call for revenge raced through this village southwest of the capital and echoed from the loudspeakers of mosques last week as the military invaded two protest camps in Cairo, killing hundreds of supporters of the deposed president, Mohamed Morsi.

"El-Sisi is killing our children," a man screamed, referring to Egypt's defense minister, Gen. Abdul-Fattah el-Sisi. "Muslims, come out of your homes!"

Hundreds of Islamists poured into the street, torching, looting and smashing the village's two churches and a nearby monastery, lashing out so ferociously that marble altars were left in broken heaps on the floor.

Over the next few days, a wave of similar attacks on the Coptic Christian minority washed over the country as Islamists set upon homes and churches, shops and schools, youth clubs and at least one orphanage, killing at least three people, according to an Egyptian human rights group. As Christians were scapegoated for supporting the military ouster of Mr. Morsi, the authorities stood by and watched: in Nazla, as in other places, the army and the police made no attempt to intervene. Few Christians in Nazla expected an investigation into the attacks.

A police station in the area had been attacked before the churches. Ebraam Sami, who lives near one of the gutted churches, said fire trucks appeared on the edge of the town, but never entered. "They said it was difficult," he said.

Leaders of the Muslim Brotherhood, the Islamist party that propelled Mr. Morsi to power, encouraged or tolerated incitement against Christians at their sit-ins, but they have started belatedly to condemn the attacks. And the military-backed government, which has done little to protect Christians, is trying to capitalize on the church burnings to paint the Brotherhood as terrorists.

Nazla and other Egyptian villages and cities have been left to cope with the war between the Islamists and the military, as politics rekindles sectarian violence that has long troubled the country. And Egypt's Coptic Christians — discriminated against and marginalized under President Hosni Mubarak, and alarmed as Islamists have won elections over the last two years — have suddenly found themselves more threatened than before.

At its churches on Monday, Christians here said they had spent days in their homes, after recognizing some of their neighbors in the attacking mobs.

The Rev. Maged Wadie Riyad, the pastor of an evangelical church in the nearby village of Zerby, which was also looted last week, said Mr. Morsi's government had intensified decades of tensions between Egypt's Muslim majority and Christians, who make up roughly 10 percent of the population.

"We don't have the culture of tolerance, or accepting one another, especially in the rural areas," Mr. Riyad said. Mr. Morsi, who never visited a church during his year as president — even after episodes of combustible intercommunal violence — "widened the gap," the pastor said.

Somehow, no one was killed in the attacks on the churches in Zerby or in Nazla, where early-morning services at one church had ended about an hour before the mob arrived.

Elsewhere, the violence took a toll. Farther south in Minya, where at least three people were killed, days of violence only quieted on

Sunday, according to Ishaq Ibrahim, who tracks attacks on Christians for the Egyptian Initiative for Personal Rights, in Cairo.

The days after the authorities stormed the Morsi supporters' encampments in Cairo "were very tough," Mr. Ibrahim said. "There were a series of attacks on churches, schools, civic organizations, orphanages and monasteries. Almost everything that had to do with the church," he said.

Among the dead were two security guards who worked on a tour boat owned by Christians and were burned to death, he said.

A Coptic Christian group, the Maspero Youth Union, recorded at least six deaths and the destruction of at least 38 churches, as well as attacks on at least 23 more. An activist with the group, Beshoy Tamry, primarily blamed Islamist leaders for "charging their followers with hate" and trying to destabilize the country by attacking its weakest citizens. The government, though, was hardly blameless, he said.

"I think the state wasn't serious about protecting churches," Mr. Tamry said. "They know who is going to do what, especially in Minya. The attacks have happened before."

Religious leaders have made little attempt to calm tensions. On Monday, a Brotherhood spokesman, Ahmed Aref, played down any culpability by the Islamist movement, blaming "foolish boys" for carrying out the attacks on the churches and the security services for failing to prevent them, suggesting a conspiracy. "It is burning with cunningness," he said in a statement.

And in recent days, the leadership of the Coptic Church has embraced the military's narrative of the conflict, praising the security forces in their fight against "terrorism" and blaming foreign news media for misreporting events.

The signs of trouble started to appear in Nazla about two weeks before the attack, when Mr. Sami and many of the almost 300 Christian families in the village started to see graffiti on their homes. On his house, the writing said: "We'll protect legitimacy with our blood," a mantra of Mr. Morsi's supporters, who have insisted that he be restored to power.

The first attack was on the Church of the Virgin Mary, which opened in April after local Christians spent 13 years collecting money and building a church, a school, a youth center and a wedding hall. Atef Hosni, who works at the church, said the rampage seemed unplanned. He stood in the sooty remains of a computer lab, picking through the debris. "This room didn't have anything to do with belief," he said.

The mob moved on, torching the village's old church, built in the 1930s, and a nearby monastery, where heat from the fire bent steel girders that once held up a roof.

At the same time, a crowd was attacking Christian homes and shops in Zerby, before arriving at Mr. Riyad's church, St. Demiana's. "They broke through the gates and stole whatever they could," he said. "What they couldn't steal, they burned."

In the chaos, there was a moment of hope. Mr. Riyad said a Muslim resident stepped in and challenged the mob, "saying if they burned it, they should burn him as well."

His actions saved the church from total destruction, the pastor said.

Mayy El Sheikh contributed reporting. A version of this article appears in print on August 21, 2013, on page A10 of the New York edition with the headline: Islamists Step Up Attacks on Christians for Supporting Morsi's Ouster.

These examples of Christian persecutions, the war on Christians, continue. This is another of the many examples reported on wordpress.com by BosNewsLife Africa Service:

Jos, Nigeria: Islamic fighters have shot dead Christians in a roadside ambush near Nigeria's central city of Jos, church representatives said. Monday, September 2.

Those killed in the attack, four kilometers (2.5 miles) off the Jos-Barkin Kadi Highway, were members of a Church of Christ in Nations (COCIN) congregation in the nearby town of Foron, according to church officials. The Christians had been ordered out of a minibus and forced to lay on the ground before being shot last Thursday, August 29, because of their faith, the COCIN denomination leadership and a witness said. Those killed were identified as Pam Gyang, 33, Felix John, 32, as well as Jimmy Tiger, 28, Ishaku Gyang, 40, and Dachung Monday, 20. Christian news agency Morning Star News quoted the local pastor Pam Jang Pam as saying that the assailants "were a combined band of ethnic Fulani herdsmen and Islamic extremist mercenaries."

Also wounded, he added, were two other as yet unidentified Christians, including a pregnant woman. Technical school student Emmanuel Sunday, who said he rode his motorbike near the murder scene, told media that he had seen the Christians and that gunmen stopped him to ask about his religion."When I told them I was a Christian, they asked me to join a group of people already ordered to lie down by the side of the road. I did as I was ordered to do, and then one of the men came and searched me and took money from me, including my mobile phone," Morning Star News quoted him as saying."It was when the gunmen started shooting and killing those of us that were Christians grouped together that I ran into a nearby maize farm, because it was already dark. They shot wildly at me, but I escaped unhurt, except the injuries I sustained while running in the bush."He said God helped him escaped to tell the story and "show the miracle" in his life. End of article.

Listed below are brief examples of the continuing war against Christians. Although these examples seem many, they are only a few. The events are too many too list even a quarter or half. These are only representative:

March 2014 in Nigeria, Armed Muslims raid a series of Christian villages, burning churches and killing sixteen, including women and four children.

March 2014 in Somalia, a woman and her cousin are beheaded in front of her young children for being Christians.

February 2014 in Nigeria, Boko Haram Islamists burn churches and massacre nearly forty people, including students at a Christian seminary.

February 2014 in Nigeria, Three catholic nuns are feared dead after their church is torched by Islamists.

February 2014 in Benghazi, Seven Christians are shot execution-style by Muslims who first confirmed their identity.

February 2014 in Egypt, A 6-year-old girl is among a Christian family of four found murdered.

February 2014 in Egypt, Three Christian tourists and their driver are killed as Shahid suicide bomber detonates a bomb on board their bus.

February 2014 in Nigeria, Over one-hundred mostly Christian villagers are rounded up and summarily hacked to death by militants shouting praises to Allah.

February 2014 in Pakistan, Muslim cops arrest an innocent Christian father of two and torture him to death.

February 2014 in Bangui, Muslims target a Christian man carrying wood, slitting his throat

February 2014 in Sudan, A Christian is killed, and two others badly burned, in a targeted bombing on their village by the Islamic Republic of Sudan.

January 2014 in Nigeria, A pastor is among eleven people slain by pro-Sharia activists.

January 2014 in Nigeria, Seven members of a Christian family are murdered in their own home by Muslim gunmen.

January 2014 in Iraq, Three Christians are shot to death by Muslim terrorists.

January 2014 in Cairo, Islamic extremists gun down a guard at a church.

January 2014 in Nigeria, Fifty-three people at a church service are slaughtered by pro-Sharia gunmen.

January 2014 in Nigeria, Muslims fire into a Christian village, killing seven residents.

January 2014 in Nigeria, Muslim terrorists attack Christians on a Sunday morning, killing at least eight and maiming others.

January 2014 in Bangladesh, Islamists murder a young Catholic man for organizing a demonstration against anti-Christian violence.

January 2014 in Syria, Two Christians are kidnaped and beheaded by Religion of Peace extremists.

January 2014 in Syria, A Christian is executed for refusing to convert to Islam.

January 2014 in Syria, A young Christian is beheaded after Islamists discover him wearing a cross necklace.

January 2014 in Bangladesh, Eight Catholics are injured during a targeted attack by Islamic extremists.

October 4, 2013 in Islamabad, Pakistan: two Christian teens and their uncle are badly beaten in their own home for refusing to embrace Islam.

September 8, 2013 in Zangang, Nigeria: a Muslim militia attack a Christian village, hacking to death fifteen residents and burning down their homes.

September 26, 2013 in Dorawa, Nigeria: A Pastor and his son are among three people machine-gunned by Religion of Peace enthusiasts.

September 25, 2013 in Derma, Libya: two Christians are invited to embrace Islam, then tied up and shot when they refuse.

September 25, 2013 in Wajir, Kenya: al-Shabaab claims credit for a grenade attack near a Catholic church.

September 22, 2013 in Peshawar, Pakistan: two Jundullah suicide bombers obliterate over eighty-five worshipers at a church service, including many women and children.

September 14, 2013 in Karachi, Pakistan: A Christian's throat is slit on the street after being branded an 'infidel' and blasphemer.

September 13, 2013 in Zanzibar, Tanzania: Muslims throw acid on a priest, badly burning him.

September 12, 2013 in Sahel Selim, Egypt: two Copts are shot to death for refusing to pay Jizya to Muslims.

September 10, 2013 in Dalga, Egypt: A 60-year-old Copt is killed while defending his home from a Muslim mob.

September 8, 2013 in Maaloula, Syria: three Christians are murdered in their home, and six others taken hostage by Islamists.

September 7, 2013 in Maaloula, Syria: at least three Christians are shot to death after declining an offer to embrace Islam.

September 4, 2013 in Maalula, Syria: Islamists slit the throat of a Christian for refusing to deny his faith, then taunted his fiancee.

September 3, 2013 in Kunte-Karu Nigeria: A brutal assault by Muslim militia on the home of a Christian family leaves six members dead, including a 7-year-old child.

September 1, 2013 in Adu, Nigeria: Nine Christian villagers, including two children, are machine-gunned in their own homes by Muslim terrorists.

August 29, 2013 in Jos, Nigeria: five Christians are ordered off a bus and summarily executed by Religion of Peace activists.

August 25, 2013 in Nasarawa, Nigeria: thirty Muslims attack a church armed with knives and clubs.

August 18, 2013 in Minya, Egypt: Islamists butcher two security guards on a boat owned by Christians.

August 17, 2013 in Minya, Egypt: A Copt survives a brutal stabbing by Muslims while trying to put out a fire at a church.

August 17, 2013 in al-Hasan, Syria: fifteen Christian villagers are reportedly massacred by Sunni terrorists.

August 17, 2013 in Homs, Syria: six Christians are murdered by Sunni terrorists.

August 17, 2013 in Sohag, Egypt: A civilian is killed while trying to defend a church from the Muslim Brotherhood.

August 16, 2013 in Alexandria, Egypt: Muslim radicals pull a Christian taxi driver out of his cab and decapitate him.

Auguts 15, 2013 in Minya, Egypt: two Copts are killed and dozens more injured when Muslim Brotherhood supporters go on a church-burning rampage.

August 14, 2013 in Raqqa, Syria: An Italian priest is kidnaped and murdered by Islamists.

August 12, 2013 in Qusayr, Syria: A young Christian girl is reportedly raped, tortured and murdered by Jihadis.

August 6, 2013 in Jaramana, Syria: Islamists set off a powerful car bomb in a Christian suburb, killing at least eighteen people.

August 6, 2013 in Ain Shams, Egypt: A 10-year-old Christian girl is shot through the heart in front of her church by pro-Muslim Brotherhood activists.

The list of Muslim atrocities (war) against Christians goes on and on. The list is endless. These events are others reported by another source:

Baghdad, Iraq: Holy Warriors target a market in a Christian area, killing at least eleven patrons in two blasts.

Daraa, Syria: Twelve people are reported killed when Islamists shell a church distributing aid to the needy.

Gwol, Nigeria: Four very young children are among a family of Christians massacred in their own home by Fulani militants.

Arboko, Nigeria: Islamists attack a Christian village, slaughtering four inhabitants and burning on-hundred homes.

Bangui, Central African Republic (CAR): A Bible translator is shot and killed by Christian-seeking Muslims.

Homs, Syria: The bodies of seven Christians are found brutally tortured and beheaded by Islamist 'rebels'.

Bangui, CAR: Three pastors, including a father of eleven, are murdered in a Muslim rampage.

Minya, Egypt: 14 Muslims rampage through a Christian village, burning homes and throwing children from roofs.

Karachi, Pakistan: A convert to Shiism is beheaded by Sunni radicals, who then hang his head from a bridge.

Barkin Ladi, Nigeria: Thirty-seven Christians in four villages are slaughtered by Muslim raiders. The dead included children and pregnant women shot at close range.

Mosul, Iraq: A Christian journalist is gunned down in a targeted attack.

Kuka, Nigeria: Five residents of a Christian village are shot dead by Muslim terrorists.

Damascus, Syria: Terrorists send a shell into a Christian neighborhood, killing two residents.

Ashigashia, Cameroon: Islamic extremists murder a Protestant missionary and set several churches ablaze.

Damascus, Syria: Nine children are reportedly crushed to death when an Islamist mortar round hits a Christian school.

Ashrafieh, Syria: Six children are killed when Islamic 'rebels' fire a rocket into a Christian neighborhood.

Sadad, Syria: The bodies of six more Christians are found. The victims were of the same family and included teens and two elderly members.

Rantis, Nigeria: Two young boys, ages 2 and 4, are among a family of Christians massacred in their home by militant Muslims.

Gilgal, Tanzania: Religion of Peace proponents hack a young man to death at a church service.

Sadad, Syria: The bodies of thirty Christian civilians are found in a mass grave from a 10-21-2013 massacre by Islamists.

Mosul, Iraq: A Christian woman is shot to death in her own home by Muslim extremists.

Haffar, Syria: At least thirteen innocents are slain when Islamists assault two Christian villages.

Mombasa, Kenya: Islamic radicals shoot a Christian pastor in the head as he is preparing a Bible study.

Warraq, Egypt: Muslim radicals open fire at church, murdering the pastor, one woman and two young girls.

Kilif, Kenya: Muslims pull a Pentecostal church cleric into the bushes and strangle him.

Mogadishu, Somalia: Islamists murder a father of five young children for spreading his Christian faith.

Baghdad, Iraq: Islamists set off a bomb in a Christian neighborhood, killing at least eight residents.

Jaramana, Syria: Eleven people are killed when Sunni terrorists fire mortars into a Christian neighborhood.

Do these tortures and murders of Christians have any source of meaning. Perhaps these three Bible quotes explain these horrible events happening to Christians. Perhaps it could be classified 'Prophetic Fulfillment:'

John 16:2
"yea the time cometh, that whosoever killeth you will think that he doeth God service."

Matthew 24:8-9 :

"But all these things are merely the beginning of birth pangs. "Then they will deliver you to tribulation, and will kill you, and you will be hated by all nations because of My name."

Revelation 6:9-11 :

"When the Lamb broke the fifth seal, I saw underneath the altar the souls of those who had been slain because of the word of God, and because of the testimony which they had maintained; and they cried out with a loud voice, saying, "How long, O Lord, holy and true, will You refrain from judging and avenging our blood on those who dwell on the earth?" And there was given to each of them a white robe; and they were told that they should rest for a little while longer, until the number of their fellow servants and their brethren who were to be killed even as they had been, would be completed also."

(When those souls who asked this question are judged from their 'Book of Life' this is known as the 'Second Resurrection.' The 'First Resurrection' is for those who refused to accept the 'mark of the beast.' According to the Bible, they will reign with Christ during the thousand years (the millennium) before all others are judged from the Book of Life.)

Chapter 9

Will U.S. Fire on U.S. Citizens?

Will government forces fire on their fellow citizens - these Christians and others who will be proclaimed 'terrorists' by our government? Yes - absolutely; and there are past examples. Consider only two; David Koresh and Randy Weaver.

This note from Wikipedia briefly describes that David Koresh (Branch Davidians) incident:

"David Koresh (born Vernon Wayne Howell; August 17, 1959 – April 19, 1993) was the American leader of the Branch Davidians religious sect, believing himself to be its final prophet. Howell legally changed his name to David Koresh on May 15, 1990 (Koresh being the Persian name of Cyrus the Great; Kurosh). A 1993 raid by the U.S. Bureau of Alcohol, Tobacco, Firearms and Explosives, and the subsequent siege by the FBI ended with the burning of the Branch Davidian ranch outside of Waco, Texas, in McLennan County. Koresh, 54 other adults, and 28 children were found dead after the fire." Neither Koresh nor any of his followers had been clearly charged with a crime."

The government took its deadly action against this group on the basis of something they thought the group had done illegally, or might be a menace to do something against the government in the future. Simply, they were considered a threat by our U.S. government. The Dividians refused to surrender when they were surrounded by armed agents because obviously they were fearful of the results. The government never explained why they surrounded the compound for so long. Just imagine the fear and agony of those 28 children during that time.

Was it really a Christian group? In their view, they were Christians trying to survive against a world they considered against them. They certainly were not 'terrorists' and had expressed no indications of harming the government. From their comments and expressed actions, they were merely a group of individuals seeking their way to personal salvation. Perhaps they were misled by Koresh in their path to salvation, but they showed no indications of being anti-government.

Perhaps this was one of the first deadly actions from our government that refused to accept thoughts and beliefs other than those the government approved. Perhaps this was the beginning of the stronger government laws and activities against free speech and thought. Now, everything one says is scrutinized and evaluated for its politically-correctness and its lawfulness. If the government doesn't like it they pass a law against it or the president signs an executive order against it - turning ordinary citizens into criminals. No doubt - this is the beginning of George Orwell's 'thought police.'

History.com gives a summary of the Randy Weaver - Ruby Ridge incident:

"In the second day of a standoff at Randy Weaver's remote northern Idaho cabin, FBI sharpshooter Lon Horiuchi wounds Randy Weaver, Kevin Harrison, and kills Weaver's wife, Vicki.

Randy Weaver, a white separatist, had been targeted by the federal government after failing to appear in court to face charges related to his selling of two illegal sawed-off shotguns to an Alcohol, Tobacco and Firearms (ATF) informant. On August 21, 1992, after a period of surveillance, U.S. marshals came upon Harrison; Weaver; Weaver's 14-year-old son, Sammy; and the family dog, Striker, on a road near the Weaver property. A marshal shot and killed the dog, prompting Sammy to fire at the marshal. In the ensuing gun battle, Sammy and U.S. Marshal Michael Degan were shot and killed. A tense standoff ensued, and on August 22 the FBI joined the marshals besieging Ruby Ridge.

Later that day, Harris, Weaver, and his daughter, Sarah, left the cabin, allegedly for the purpose of preparing Sammy's body for burial. FBI sharpshooter Lon Horiuchi, waiting 200 yards away, opened fire, allegedly because he thought Harrison was armed and intending to fire on a helicopter in the vicinity. Horiuchi wounded Weaver, and the group ran to the shed where Sammy's body was lying. When they attempted to escape back into the cabin, Horiuchi fired again, wounding Harrison as he dove through the door and killing Vicki Weaver, who was holding the door open with one hand and cradling her infant daughter with the other. Horiuchi claimed he didn't know that Vicki Weaver was standing behind the door. Harris, Weaver, and Weaver's three daughters surrendered nine days later.

In 1993, Weaver and Harris were acquitted by a federal court on murder, conspiracy, and other charges related to Degan's death, but Weaver was convicted of failing to appear for trial on the firearms charge. In 1994, the two men filed federal civil rights cases against the FBI and U.S. marshals stemming from the siege, and in 1995 the government settled Weaver's case for $3.1 million."

The incident was instigated by the agents. They didn't know the trial date had been changed to a later date. As a result of their actions, innocent people were killed by the government.

Would our government agents hesitate to fire on terrorists if ordered to do so by our government leaders? How soon and under what conditions will many Christians be proclaimed 'terrorists' by a tyrannical government? How could our government troops refuse to fire? Perhaps this was the meaning of the warning in Revelation for believers to 'flee to the wilderness.'

Perhaps this next article by Todd Starnes from Townhall.com, October 28, 2013, might help answer that question, "Would our government ever fire on American citizens?" How easy it would be for a tyrannical government to categorize any group or any individual as terrorist - and order government troops to fire on them. Would American troops fire on their own citizenry? Too many similar examples exist to suggest they would.

This is that information from Todd Starnes. It's titled: 'Army Briefing Labels Tea Party, Christians as Terror Threats:'

"Soldiers attending a pre-deployment briefing at Fort Hood say they were told that evangelical Christians and members of the Tea Party were a threat to the nation and that any soldier donating to those groups would be subjected to punishment under the Uniform Code of Military Justice.

A soldier who attended the Oct.17th briefing told me the counter-intelligence agent in charge of the meeting spent nearly a half hour discussing how evangelical Christians and groups like the American Family Association were "tearing the country apart."

Michael Berry, an attorney with the Liberty Institute, is advising the soldier and has launched an investigation into the incident.

"The American public should be outraged that the U.S. Army is teaching our troops that evangelical Christians and Tea Party members are enemies of America, and that they can be punished for supporting or participating in those groups," said Berry, a former Marine Corps JAG officer.

"These statements about evangelicals being domestic enemies are a serious charge."

The soldier told me he fears reprisals and asked not to be identified. He said there was a blanket statement that donating to any groups that were considered a threat to the military and government was punishable under military regulations.

"My first concern was if I was going to be in trouble going to church," the evangelical Christian soldier told me. "Can I tithe? Can I donate to Christian charities? What if I donate to a politician who is a part of the Tea Party movement?"

Another soldier who attended the briefing alerted the Chaplain Alliance for Religious Liberty. That individual's recollections of the briefing matched the soldier who reached out to me.

"I was very shocked and couldn't believe what I was hearing," the soldier said. "I felt like my religious liberties, that I risk my life and sacrifice time away from family to fight for, were being taken away."

And while a large portion of the briefing dealt with the threat evangelicals and the Tea Party pose to the nation, barely a word was said about Islamic extremism, the soldier said.

"Our community is still healing from the act of terrorism brought on by Nidal Hasan – who really is a terrorist," the soldier said. "This is a slap in the face. "The military is supposed to defend freedom and to classify the vast majority of the military that claim to be Christian as terrorists is sick." (Author note: Nidal Hasan was not identified as an Islamic terrorist by Barack Obama. The Muslim creed is that: 'a good Muslim is one who does no harm to another Muslim by mouth or by hand.')

Tony Perkins, president of the Family Research Council, tells me the Pentagon is pushing anti-Christian propaganda.

"On the very base that was the site of mass murder carried out by a radicalized Muslim soldier, it is astonishing that it is evangelical groups that are being identified as a 'threat,'" he said. "Defense Secretary Chuck Hagel must immediately intervene to stop this march against the rights and freedom of our soldiers."

The soldier said they were also told that the pro-life movement is another example of "radicalization."

"They said that evangelical Christians protesting abortions are the mobilization stage and that leads to the bombing of abortion clinics," he said, recalling the discussion.

An Army spokesman at the Pentagon tells me they do not maintain or publish a list of organizations considered extremist.

"None of these slides [shown at the briefing] were produced by the Army, but by soldiers who included information found during an Internet search," the spokesman said.

He said commanders and other leaders were cautioned that they should not use "lists of extremists, hate groups, radical factions or the like compiled by any outside non-governmental groups or organizations for briefings, command presentations, or as a short cut to determining if a group or activity is considered to be extremist."

Meanwhile, the public affairs office at Fort Hood is denying the soldiers' allegations.

"The allegations you are asking about were brought to the attention of the Fort Hood leadership immediately and a (sic) inquiry is occurring," read a statement from Tom Rheinlander, the public affairs director at Fort Hood. "At this time, initial information gathered about the training and what you claim occurred is not substantiated by unit leadership and soldiers present at this training venue."

I sent the public affairs officer additional questions about the specific content of the briefing but he declined to respond.

But this is not the first time an Army briefing has labeled evangelicals as extremists. Last April an Army Reserve briefing classified Evangelical Christianity and Catholicism as "religious extremism."

In a letter to Rep. Doug Lamborn (R-Colo.), Secretary of the Army John McHugh said the briefing in April was an isolated incident and the material used was not sanctioned by the Army. McHugh said it was a "misguided attempt to explain that extremism is not limited to a single religion."

Two weeks ago, several dozen active duty troops at Camp Shelby in Mississippi, were told the American Family Association, a well-respected Christian ministry, should be classified as a domestic hate group because it advocates for traditional family values.

Again, the military called it an isolated incident with a trainer using material that was not sanctioned by the military.

That explanation is wearing thin with American Christians.

"How much longer can the Army claim no knowledge or responsibility for these things?" Berry asked.

"These repeated incidents show either that this training was directed from Army leadership at the Pentagon, or else the Army has a real discipline and leadership problem on its hands because a bunch of rogue soldiers are teaching this nonsense."

The most recent allegations at Fort Hood have drawn sharp rebuke from religious liberty groups around the nation.

"Why is the Army engaged in these anti-Christian training propaganda briefings?" asked Perkins, himself a veteran of the Marine Corps. "The only explanation is that this is a deliberate effort of the Obama administration to intimidate and separate soldiers from Christian groups that they support and that support them."

Ron Crews, executive director of the Chaplain Alliance, called the military's behavior dishonorable.

"Far from mere 'isolated incidents,' as the Army has dismissed previous occurrences, this latest incident demonstrates a pattern and practice of Army briefings identifying mainstream religions, such as Evangelical Christianity, Judaism, and Catholicism, as examples of 'religious extremism' similar to Al Qaeda, Hamas and the Ku Klux Klan," he told me.

Perkins said it's time for the Pentagon to "ensure that instructors carry out their role to train our troops to defend our freedom, and not push anti-Christian propaganda." End of article.

Not only are Christians being identified and proclaimed as terrorists and others who mean harm to 'their America,' others whom the leftist consider against their Socialist and Communist plans are also being identified and targeted. Generally, anyone who disagrees with them have labels such as 'terrorist' and 'anarchist' cast at them. In this category, Republicans are their general targets; Tea party members are their more specific targets. This report by CNSNews.com, on August 14, 2014 reports one specific example:

(CNSNews.com) – Hollywood director and liberal activist Rob Reiner told talk-show host Larry King that the Tea Party is like the terrorist group Hamas, because apparently both groups are extreme and cannot be negotiated with, and the only solution is to make them go away or "eliminate" them.

"You can't negotiate with that, you have to say either Hamas goes away and the Palestinian authority takes over all that region and deal with some kind of honest broker here, and create the two-state solution," said Reiner.

Drawing a parallel with the Tea Party, he said, "anytime you're dealing with an extreme group, you cannot negotiate with them, and the way to do it is to eliminate it. With the Tea Party, you have to go through the political thing, you have to wait till 2020 to redistrict, but that is really tough stuff."

On the Aug. 14 edition of Politicking with Larry King, the host asked Reiner, "What's to do about the Gaza situation, and Israel?"

Reiner said, "Well, there again, you've got a horrible situation where you have an extreme faction, the Hamas, that controls Gaza, that is written into their playbook, the destruction of Israel, the destruction of every Jew on the planet."

"You can't negotiate with that," he said, "you have to say either Hamas goes away and the Palestinian authority takes over all that region and deal with some kind of honest broker here, and create the two-state solution."

"The Palestinians turned down the ability to have their own state in 1948 when Israel was formed, so clearly, Hamas, and again, the virulent faction of a, really, uh, group can control everything," said the

Academy Award nominee.

Reiner continued, "You look at the Congress right now in the United States, you've got a strong Tea Party group controlling the whole country, because they have a gridlock, they have a gridlock, stranglehold on Boehner. Boehner can't make a move, and so for that reason, nothing gets brought up in the Congress."

"So anytime you're dealing with an extreme group, you cannot negotiate with them, and the way to do it is to eliminate it," said Reiner. "With the Tea Party, you have to go through a political thing, you have to wait till 2020 to redistrict, but, uh, that is really tough stuff."

The U.S. State Department designated Hamas a terrorist organization in 1997. The Tea Party stands for Taxed Enough Already and sprang up from the American grassroots in 2010 largely in opposition to Obamacare, and has broadened to include issues such limited government, fewer government regulations, and adherence to the Constitution. End of article.

Forwardprogressives.com adds more in an article titled: 'It's Time to be Honest: The Tea Party Has Become a Terrorist Group.' April 16, 2014 By Allen Clifton:

"While I'm sure many liberals who come across this headline will have some response like "Duh" or "Tell me something I didn't already know, " I think it's time to put hyperbole aside and get real for a moment.

Sure, for a while many liberals have called tea party supporters domestic terrorists and have accused them of actively trying to sabotage our government. And with valid reasons – they have been trying to blatantly sabotage our government ever since President Obama moved into the White House.

They've done everything possible to hold our country back economically, threatened to force our country to default on our debt for the first time in history, shut down the government and have wasted millions of taxpayer dollars blatantly trying to sabotage the Affordable Care Act.

But as time goes on, more of these tea party politicians are speaking out against civil rights (even suggesting the Civil Rights Act is unconstitutional), pushing for laws that allow for religious discrimination and the anti-government rhetoric continues to expand within the Republican party.

Take for instance the escalating standoff in Nevada where anti-government activists came armed, talked about a strategy to use women as human shields, and Cliven Bundy apparently brought in his whole family (including his 54 grandchildren) to his location in anticipation of possible government action against him for violating federal law.

Because nothing says "good family values" quite like putting your children and grandchildren in harms way while your supporters considered using women as human shields if federal officers decided to enforce federal laws.

And while the situation in Nevada is an extreme instance of anti-government lunacy being represented by these far-right

Republicans, I'm seeing more and more people rally in support of such radical, and potentially deadly, actions.

While there's always been those nut jobs tucked away in the most insane corners of our country who hoard guns and "prepare" for the overthrow of the government, these people are now pushing their way into the mainstream with politicians who are actually representing their delusional beliefs. (Author's note: a comment on the view of 'preppers' and guns is included in the next chapter.)

These people have a sole purpose of destroying all the progress we've made in this country. Their main goal is to oppose anything and everything related to the federal government because they've been brainwashed into believing that the government is some evil boogeyman that's out to get them.

These are the people who years ago were seen as the "tinfoil hat" people, yet with the emergence of the tea party, they've now been given a voice. But add into the equation the fact that they basically hate anyone who isn't a straight white Christian male.

Could you imagine if a group of Middle Eastern Muslims was armed on some ranch threatening federal officers? Then imagine if one of these people admitted that they were planning to use women as a human shield. Conservatives would be freaking out. Instead, many of them are looking to Bundy as some kind of anti-government hero. End of article.

Next is an article from breitbart.com, reported by Joel B. Pollak on 7 July 2014. It describes another attack on the Tea Party:

"The "Tequila Party," a Latino group formed in opposition to the Tea Party, wrote to U.S. Attorney General Eric Holder and FBI Director James Comey on Monday to request that the Tea Party and several officials be investigated for their role in protesting and blocking the transfer of illegal aliens captured in Texas to Murrieta, California. The protests on July 1 turned back three busloads of aliens, though more are scheduled to arrive.

In their letter--signed by California attorney Ruben Salazar, pro-amnesty activist Dee Dee Garcia Blase, and Nebraska attorney Shirl Mora James--the group, writing on the letterhead of a new organization called "Somos Independents," called on Holder and Comey to launch an "outside investigation" of Murrieta city councilwoman Diana Serafin; U.S. Customs and Border Patrol agents Steven Golda and Gabe Pacheo; Murrieta mayor Alan Long, protest leader Patrice Lynes; the Murrieta Police Department, and local resident Joseph Culberson.

In addition, the signatories accuse Tea Party activists in Murrieta of being "homeland domestic terrorists (masquerading as patriots)," and allege that they were "were obstructing federal law enforcement from performing their jobs and terrorizing small refugee immigrant children from Central America with racial slurs."

Update: Blase responded to a request by Breitbart News for further comment. In response to a question about whether the activists expected the Department of Justice to respond to the request, Blase said:

"I believe the DOJ will respond to all written formal requests of concern regarding Civil Rights issues. Please recall when Sheriff Joe

Arpaio was investigated due to public outcry, and when Thomas E. Perez, assistant attorney general at the Department's Civil Rights Division said at a news conference: "At its core, this is an abuse-of-power case involving a sheriff and sheriff's office that disregarded the Constitution, ignored sound police practices, compromised public safety and did not hesitate to retaliate against his perceived critics." End of article.

This is another article on ivn.us, reported by W.E. Messamore on August 3, 2011:

"Members of the Tea Party movement have been called a lot of nasty things before like: crazy, extremists, teabaggers, and racists, but in the final hours of the debt ceiling debate, just one month before the ten-year anniversary of the 9-11 terrorist attacks, many Democrats, including Vice President Joe Biden, have been calling Tea Party members the nastiest name yet: terrorists.

Sources in the room told The Politico that in a closed-door meeting of House Democrats with Vice President Joe Biden, Rep. Mike Doyle (D-PA) said:

"We have negotiated with terrorists. This small group of terrorists have made it impossible to spend any money… "the Tea Party acted like terrorists in threatening to blow up the economy."

After the word was thrown around by angry House Democrats, sources told The Politico that Vice President Joe Biden agreed, saying: "They have acted like terrorists." Biden's office initially declined to remark on what he had said in the meeting, but after the comment was published, a Biden spokeswoman issued a denial, saying:

"The word was used by several members of Congress. The vice president does not believe it's an appropriate term in political discourse."

In an interview with CBS News, Biden also denied using "the terrorism word," but told his interviewer that he said "if" Tea Party members were terrorists, the "nuclear weapon" has been taken out of their hands. But remember that despite Biden's (rather weak) denial, The Politico's report cited multiple, Democratic sources in the room who confirmed that Biden had called Tea Party Republicans terrorists, casting an awful lot of suspicion on the vice president's denial.

In addition to "several" House Democrats as confirmed by the office of the vice president, and likely the vice president himself, members of the media have also been using the word "terrorist" in recent days to describe the Tea Party. Three days before The Politico broke the Biden story, one of its opinion columnists wrote a piece entitled "The Tea Party's Terrorist Tactics," opining:

"It has become commonplace to call the tea party faction in the House 'hostage takers.' But they have now become full-blown terrorists," adding that, "Terrorism is a tough term, but, unfortunately, it describes tea party tactics precisely."

On the day the Biden story broke, a New York Times columnist published a piece entitled "The Tea Party's War on America," which begins:

"You know what they say: Never negotiate with terrorists. It only encourages them. These last few months, much of the country has watched in horror as the Tea Party Republicans have waged jihad on the American people... Their goal, they believed, was worth blowing up the country for, if that's what it took."

The next day at Salon, as if the word "terrorist" weren't bad enough, a columnist argued that the Tea Party consists of radical, white, southern Neo-Confederates who would not hesitate to "destroy American democracy in order to get their way." This is in addition to House Democrats who have also been using the word "Satan" in describing negotiations with House Republicans, with Rep. Emanuel Cleaver (D-MO) calling the debt ceiling deal a "Satan sandwich" and House minority leader Nancy Pelosi adding "with a side of Satan fries."

As the debt ceiling debate came to a final close, Tea Party members were also called "arsonists," "saboteurs," and "extortionists" by Democratic politicians and journalists. It's sufficiently evident that the use of this new "terrorist" smear isn't merely the angry ranting of a couple amateur bloggers, but a widespread phenomenon originating at some of the highest levels in electoral politics and news media. And it's not the first time the Tea Party has been falsely and unfairly associated with acts of violence or terrorism.

This January, when a gunman in Arizona murdered six people and critically wounded Congresswoman Gabrielle Giffords (D-AZ) in a tragic shooting massacre, Democrats in the media rushed to blame the Tea Party for inciting the violence with vitriolic rhetoric. New York Times columnist Paul Krugman led the charge, blaming Republicans for fomenting "a climate of hate." Many bloggers directly accused Sarah Palin of inciting the murder attempt on Giffords with a map of targets on Democratic House districts vulnerable to Republican challenges in the 2010 midterm elections. DailyKos founder Markos

Moulitsas tweeted "Mission accomplished, Sarah Palin."

As it turned out, the rush to judgment was patently false. Despite the perverse hopes of the progressive blogosphere, the shooter wasn't a Tea Party member, a Republican, a devotee of Glenn Beck, or even a self-described conservative. His writings indicated if anything, a sympathy for progressive politics, but most of all, simply the deranged mind of a clinically insane young man. End of article.

Another article from downtrend.com, posted by Brian Carey on September 27, 2013, gives more:

"It's been a fun week of rhetoric in Washington, D.C. and New York. Liberals, in a feeble-minded effort to express themselves forcibly, have resorted to some unusually harsh language when criticizing Tea Party Republicans.

Here are the 6 dumbest things that our friends on the left have said about those House Republicans just this past week:

1. Dan Pfeiffer compared the House Republicans to terrorists with a bomb strapped to their chest.

Dan Pfeiffer is not just any liberal. He's a White House senior adviser. On CNN yesterday, he told Jake Tapper that the White House will not negotiate with House Republicans. He put it this way: "What we're not for is negotiating with people with a bomb strapped to their chest."

2. Sen. Barbara Mikulski called the Tea Party Republicans "Tea Baggers." The Democrat from Maryland really needs to grow up.

"The reason Ted Cruz stood up and asked for a delay was so that he could have a vote during today where his — the tea baggers in his tea party were going to watch," Mikulski said when asked why the cloture vote did not occur last night."

3. Sen. Harry Reid called the Tea Party Republicans "anarchists."

One would think that Sen. Reid would understand the difference between "no government" and "limited government". Apparently not.

On the Senate Floor earlier this week, Senate Majority Leader Harry Reid made it patently clear to everyone that the so-called "anarchists" comprising the Republican Party aren't going to get their way.

"We're not going to bow to tea party anarchists who deny the mere fact that Obamacare is the law. We will not bow to tea party anarchists who refuse to accept that the Supreme Court ruled that Obamacare is constitutional," Reid said in a blistering opening speech. "The simple fact remains: Obamacare is the law of the land and will remain the law of the land as long as Barack Obama is president of the United States and as long as I'm Senate majority leader."

4. Nancy Pelosi said that the House Republicans are engaging in "legislative arson."

Actually, the Tea Party Republicans are trying to put out the fire that Pelosi and her friends created. She, of course, doesn't see it that way.

"I call them 'legislative arsonists'," she said. "They're there to burn down what we should be building up in terms of investments and education and scientific research, and all that it is that makes our country great and competitive."

5. Jay Carney called the effort to defund ObamaCare an "extortion game"

What we call negotiation, they call extortion. That's the difference between Republicans and Democrats these days.

"We cannot agree to an extortion game when they attach everything on their Republican wish list or they will blow up the economy," White House spokesman Jay Carney told reporters.

6. Al Gore said that the Republicans are guilty of "political terrorism." Seems to be a common theme this week.

Former Vice President Al Gore said the GOP is guilty of "political terrorism" because of those who are threatening a government shutdown over Obamacare.

"The only phrase that describes it is political terrorism," Gore said Friday, speaking at the launch of the Brookings Institution's Center for Effective Public Management in Washington. "Why does partisanship have anything to do with such a despicable and dishonorable threat to the integrity of the United States of America?" End of article.

These articles above give expressions that strongly suggest God-fearing American citizens might one day face jeopardy and tyranny from our government. (Please read page 3 of this book.) And, that jeopardy might come from many directions. Perhaps the first has already occurred - in the form of eliminating free speech for American citizens.

Citizens are already being threatened and face jail and worse for expressing their opinions of truth. Many times, the truth offends some - but there should be no law against being offended. Our Founders made that intention in our Constitution very clear.

Does not tyranny always begin with censorship and control of communications? Clearly, that's already happening in our great nation. And, the basis of that control is even the more dangerous. It's being manipulated from two fronts:

First are the Islamists who openly say - pronounce - proclaim they will destroy our American way of life; we are 'infidels.' Should we ignore their threats - and not believe them? Perhaps not - since they are carrying out their proclaimed and written plan, their 'Agenda' right before our eyes - and our government is helping them!

Second are the proponents of the New World Order - now being enforced through Agenda 21 (Sustainable Programs) and immigration policies. When this plan is finished, we will no longer be Americans, Canadians, Bolivians, or Mexicans. We will all become 'World Citizens' with no national allegiance. Fluid immigration, without control, is merely a beginning process. It's already started on our southern borders. The undertow of this broad ambition is to create a world of a 'classless' society where everyone is equal. One of the tactics is exploitation of the 'global warming' ideology. The truth of the matter is irrelevant - the purpose is to 'control' the masses.

The man charged with the highest responsibility to protect our freedoms described in our Constitution is Barack Hussein Obama. Is he fulfilling that responsibility? What are his ulterior intentions?

Another concern about the administration's actions toward our security is that of treatment and suspicion of our veterans returning from overseas wars. Many are being identified by the government as "right-wing extremists." Returning vets were seen as vulnerable to "right-wing extremists" in an April 2009 report by Janet Napolitano's Homeland Security Dept., titled "Right-wing Extremism: Current Economic and Political Climate Fueling Resurgence in Radicalization and Recruitment:"

"Returning veterans possess combat skills and experience that are attractive to right-wing extremists," it says. "Department of Homeland Security's Office of Intelligence and Analysis is concerned that right-wing extremists will attempt to recruit and radicalize veterans in order to boost their violent capacities."

Is Obama and his administration trying to discredit our honorable veterans for another ulterior purpose - to de-mobilize them from future patriotic activities? In his 'Call to service' speech on July 2, 2008 in Colorado Springs, then presidential candidate Barack Obama said,

> "We cannot continue to rely on our military in order to achieve the national security objectives we've set. We've got to have a civilian national security force that's just as powerful, just as strong, just as well-funded."

What did he mean by that? What would be the purpose of that civilian national security force? He has never explained, but recent events suggest he is beginning to act on that plan he revealed during that speech.

Recently, the Department of Homeland Security, operating under strict Obama policies bought 1.6 billion (that's billion - with a B) rounds of high-powered ammunition, 7000 full-auto assault rifles, and 2700 armored vehicles. There's still some uncertainty about the vehicles, but the Department of Homeland Security has not revealed the purpose for the other weaponry.

Is it to be used against drug smugglers crossing our southern borders? Is it to be used against radical jihadists led by the ghost of Osama Bin Laden wading ashore at the Boardwalk in Atlantic City? Or is to be used against those rowdy grandmothers who don't win enough when they play 'Bingo' at the community center? Who are these weapons to be used against? Department of Homeland Security, just tell us an answer that makes sense. Our Founding Fathers spoke against a force such as this and said it would be dangerous to its citizens. Is it? New revelations reveal that possibility. Here's more about DHS ammunition purchases:

An article by Paul Joseph Watson, of PrisonPlanet.com on March 25, 2013 revealed that while the Department of Homeland Security continues to ignore members of Congress demanding to know why the federal agency is engaged in an apparent arms build-up, the DHS has just announced it plans to purchase another 360,000 rounds of hollow point ammunition to add to the roughly 2 billion bullets already bought over the past year.

As reported elsewhere, some of this purchase order is for hollow-point rounds, forbidden by international law for use in war, along with a frightening amount specialized for snipers. Also reported elsewhere, at the height of the Iraq War the Army was expending less than 6 million rounds a month. Therefore 1.6 billion rounds would be enough to sustain a hot war for over twenty years.

A solicitation on the Federal Business Opportunities website details the DHS' plan to purchase 360,000 rounds of "Commercial leaded training ammo (CLTA) Pistol .40 caliber 165 grain, jacketed hollow point." The bullets are to be delivered to the Federal Law Enforcement Training Center in Artesia, New Mexico, the same destination for 240,000 hollow point rounds which were purchased only last month.

Although the DHS has attempted to explain its mammoth purchase of ammunition by claiming the bullets are being acquired in bulk to save money and that they are for training purposes only, this has been disputed by reputable voices such as former Marine Richard Mason, who told reporters with WHPTV News in Pennsylvania earlier this month, "We never trained with hollow points, we didn't even see hollow points my entire four and a half years in the Marine Corps." Hollow point bullets are almost twice as expensive as full metal jackets, therefore the DHS' explanation that it is buying huge quantities in bulk to "save money" doesn't make sense.

(Author's note: For those who are not aware of the difference in hollow point bullets and regular bullets, the difference is great. Although the DHS claims these bullets are for "training purposes only" that reason is pure and blatant deception. Hollow point bullets are never used for training - and for two reasons. First, is the cost; they are much more expensive, and since the purpose for target practice is to improve one's aim, hollow points do not improve that purpose. In a normal paper target the hollow point could never be discerned. It would simply pass through a piece of paper like a finger, pencil, pen, or regular bullet.

The second reason is safety. As stated above, in a paper target it couldn't be discerned if it were a hollow point or a regular bullet. To tell the difference, a hard target must be used. And, practicing with hollow point bullets at a hard target would be too dangerous. Upon hitting a hard target the hollow point bullet expands or explodes - to create more impact and damage. Ricochets and flying fragments from the shattered bullets would spread in all directions creating a hazard zone for anyone in the immediate area.

Simply, hollow point bullets would never be used for training purposes. If the DHS is giving this reason for purchasing hollow point bullets then they are claiming that American citizens are stupid.)

According to Watson's article ,Retired United States Army Captain Terry M. Hestilow sent a letter to Sen. John Cornyn (R-TX) warning that the ammo purchases represent "a bold threat of war by that agency (DHS), and the Obama administration, against the citizens of the United States of America." Questions from members of Congress about why the federal agency is buying up ammo, exacerbating shortages across the country, have been met with silence.

 Kansas Congressman Timothy Huelscamp said last week that threats should be made to withdraw funding from the DHS if it didn't explain why it was purchasing so many bullets, remarking, "They have no answer for that question. They refuse to answer that."

Earlier this month, New Jersey Congressman Leonard Lance said, "Congress has a responsibility to ask Secretary Napolitano as to exactly why these purchases have occurred," signaling his intention to get answers.

Californian Congressman Doug LaMalfa and 14 of his House colleagues have written a letter to the Department of Homeland Security asking if the purchases are, "being conducted in a manner that strategically denies the American people access to ammunition."

Although members of Congress are treating the matter with the seriousness it deserves, the mainstream and leftist media have attempted to ridicule the entire issue as a conspiracy theory, with Atlantic Wire even suggesting that the story had its origins in a debunked email, a report that completely failed to even mention the admitted fact that the DHS had purchased around 2 billion bullets.

While the DHS continues to purchase bullets in large quantities, police departments have been forced to barter amongst each other in a desperate scramble to meet their ammo needs.

In August, 2012 the Department of Homeland Security censored information relating to the amount of bullets purchased by the DHS on behalf of Immigration & Customs Enforcement, citing an "unusual and compelling urgency" to acquire the bullets, noting that there is a shortage of bullets which is threatening a situation that could cause "substantial safety issues for the government" should law enforcement officials not be adequately armed.

But who are they arming against? Who is their enemy? It seems they are arming against those dangerous 'right wing terrorists - those returning veterans.' Perhaps many of us who respect our Constitution might also be those targets.

According to Ben Shapiro, Editor-At-Large of Breitbart News, "The attempt by the left - to minimize the threat of Islamic terror inside the

United States and to maximize the threat of 'right-wing extremism' is all too obvious. By using the label 'right-wing extremism' to apply to everything from neo-Nazis to anarchists, the left seeks to smear the right, the same way it smeared the right with the shooting of Gabrielle Giffords.

The truth remains that the Islamist threat in the United States is very real – and that only the dedication of law enforcement has stopped substantially more Islamist attacks. After the Boston Marathon bombings that killed three and wounded well over 170, only a truly philosophically perverse publication would claim that right-wingers are actually more of a threat to public safety than Islamists."

This is another comment, by the Huffington Post on April 14, 2009 regarding the supposed right-wing extremism, "If you think the conservative 'Tea Party' movement is daunting, take a look at a new report issued by the Department of Homeland Security that says right-wing extremism is on the rise throughout the country.

In the report, officials warn that right-wing extremists could use the bad state of the U.S. economy and the election of the country's first black president to recruit new members to their cause. In the intelligence assessment issued to law enforcement last week, Homeland Security officials said there was no specific information about an attack from right-wing extremists in the works.

The agency warns that an extended economic downturn with real estate foreclosures, unemployment, and an inability to obtain credit could foster an environment for extremists to recruit new members who may not have been supportive of these causes in the past."

So, who is this massive group of 'dangerous right-wing terrorists' the DHS warns us about? How is this group so dangerous DHS must order two billion rounds of ammunition, including hollow point, to stop? In almost every example they use, it's not a group who perpetuates a criminal act - of which they can classify any way they desire. Ordinarily, it's a criminal act such as bank robbery, domestic violence, racially-motivated, or settlement of a grudge. Also considered are the 'skin-heads' and neo-Nazis.' Nevertheless, the DHS has no clear and indisputable examples of 'right-wing' terrorism. End of article.

The major question remains - why is the DHS buying so many bullets - especially hollow point bullets? Could there, even in one's wildest imagination, be that many right-wing terrorists who threaten our security? Who are to be the targets of those bullets?

If this encroachment, this silent jihad, continues perhaps a time will come when the question of 'taking up arms' might be a consideration. With this ban on questioning Muslim intentions and actions in America, perhaps the day will come when they lose their patience and begin to initiate 'test' terror attacks to test our will, courage, and commitment to defend ourselves and our great 'Christian' nation.

If and when this were to occur, would these test attacks be blamed on Republicans and the Tea Party? Of course, it's unreasonable to even suggest this scenario - but is it not as unreasonable to suggest that members of one political party would proclaim the members of another party 'terrorist' and 'anarchists?' Terrorism exists only in the minds and words of those making the accusation - those with the political and military power to take action against those charged.

This brings the question: should U.S. citizens be armed? I realize I am placing myself in jeopardy by saying - Yes! Every competent U.S. citizen must own a weapon and know how to use it. However, it's not for the purpose espoused by those in government who fear an armed citizenry.

Every citizen must be armed, not from fear of having to fire on tyrannical government troops, as the government would have you believe and as they suggest. Instead, every citizen must be armed to keep from having to fire a shot. Islamic terrorists must know that every U.S. citizen takes their threats seriously - and that every citizen is prepared to put a bullet through their heads if they dare attack us. The next chapter explains this idea further.

Chapter 10

American Citizens Must be Armed

"We will destroy you terrorists; we will attack you and rid your kind that has no regard for decent human life from the face of the earth. You are not human and the religion you stand behind is not a religion - it is a theology of anti-humanity. You are, plain and simple, blatant and vicious terrorists. We will fire bullets through you and drop bombs on your head until you no longer exist."

Until Barack Obama, or any U.S. president, says these words or similar words, our great nation and the world remain in serious danger. Obama refuses to call them "terrorists." Now, he and his attorney general, Eric Holder, want to deal with these terrorist acts as 'criminal acts,' and track them down with the FBI. While Obama hides out on the golf course, Eric Holder goes to Ferguson to play the 'race card.'

All these actions and lack of actions threaten the peace, tranquility and prosperity of our great nation. Our leaders' lack of positive action against tyranny invites great danger - and it involves every private citizen. If you, as a private citizen, wait to be protected by Barack Obama and Eric Holder, it will be a great mistake. The current resolve of these terrorists is to attack and destroy America - The Great Satan. Then, the rest of the world will be an easy takeover.

We know many of them want to be martyrs: to serve their 'god' and to get those 72 virgins. (Very puzzling: if they have no body parts, why are they still looking forward to having 72 virgins - or any woman?) What does that mean? In my opinion it means they will begin as soon as possible to start instilling fear in American citizens. This will be on a small scale - not a large vicious attack as our leaders anticipate. To me, the most logical and practical plan for their purpose of instilling fear is to mount small attacks across our southern borders. Likely, their fear attacks will be across the border through tunnels - just like the ones Hamas uses to attack Israel. Those tunnels are sophisticated and well-financed. So will be those on our southern border.

So, as an ordinary citizen what should we do? We must arm ourselves - and let the terrorists throughout the world know that every citizen is armed and ready to use our weapons against them. If and when you are attacked, calling 911 might be too late to protect you and your family. Being armed and letting the world know you are armed will likely prevent that attack altogether.

As you prepare, please know that Obama and his administration are against the arming of private citizens. (Why?) Most certainly, every gun being purchased and every ammunition sale is now recorded at the NSA center in Bluffdale, Utah. Plus, in many cases the sale of ammunition is already being allocated.

If and when terrorist attacks occur, what will likely be Obama's first reaction? To stop the sale of private weapons and ammunition, and confiscate those from gun owners to 'prevent the spread of terrorism.' From an act of desperation - and one might suspect cooperation with a greater goal of the Muslim Brotherhood - those patriots trying to defend America and freedom might be the very ones listed as 'terrorists' by our government.

What would happen to unarmed citizens if only one or two Islamic terrorists blocked a major highway on a long stretch with no exits, and began walking along that highway shooting every person in every automobile? If citizens were not armed, that slaughter could continue until enough armed police arrived. How long would that take?

Now this is the pertinent and life-saving question - and the reason every competent U.S. citizen must be armed. Would terrorists even attempt such an action if they knew or suspected most of those people in the automobiles were armed and prepared to shoot them? I think not.

In this dangerous world threatened by ungodly Islamic terrorists - and others, we must be armed. Our government must not be allowed to prevent us from getting our weapons of defense - and they must not be allowed to confiscate them under any pretenses.

One of those pretenses is the claim that many 'anarchist citizens' are hoarding guns and ammunition to defend themselves against a tyrannical government. They consider the 'preppers' part of those anarchists. In reality, even the preppers know they could not defend themselves against the forces of government. That is totally out of the question and an unreasonable consideration.

The preppers are positioning to defend themselves and their families against two aggressive possibilities. One is against radical Islamic terrorists who might invade their area. The other threat they try to guard against are the roving bands of marauders who might be reactionary to an oppressive government's actions against common citizens. These marauders would be seeking food and other items of survival if and when disenfranchised by the government. Preppers actions are purely to defend and protect themselves and their families - not to participate in revolution against the government. But - this will be the logical excuse the government will employ when they try to confiscate those weapons.

Conclusion

Born from chaos and bathed in hope, America rose as a dim star on the night's horizon. From the European point of view, America bloomed as a new source of revenue and prosperity. For the bold new immigrants, America was a new beginning; a beginning of freedom and hope, an escape from total despair and depression. America burst from the night's busy sky to establish a bright new vision for humanity.

That beginning wasn't easy or predestined. It took visionary leaders of courage and wisdom not only to create that vision, but also to take the first bold steps. They sacrificed everything to give those who would come after them un-imagined freedom and opportunity. They saw only a future of prosperity, caring, decency, and fellowship for those later citizens.

America was on its way; almost there to the end of those founders' dream. Then it happened; American citizens changed their aspirations, and that dream was abandoned. Their aspirations changed from 'let me do more' to 'let me have more.' Those early dreamers who sacrificed for America's future are certainly looking down, tears flowing from their eyes as they realize America is returning to Europe, and perhaps beyond. November 6, 2012 was the day America died. What happened?

With such high hopes and dreams for the future of America, in the early beginning and after World War II, how is it possible that dream slipped away? Did it merely slip away or was the dream suddenly jerked from the vision of those expecting the dream to last forever?

Or, was the idea of America as a special place merely an idea or a dream and not reality? Perhaps from the beginning America was destined to reach a high point and then deteriorate as have all other countries and empires before. Was the concept that America would be the 'melting pot' of the world a plus or a minus for the longevity of the great nation? Maybe America wasn't special after all. Maybe America was merely just another idea fulfilling its transitory place in history.

Even as we look to history for an answer, there is no clear and perfect answer as to what has happened to America. America doesn't fit any historical model, because technology and communications have been such a recent revolution. Throughout history, when a person immigrated to another country or alien area, that person ordinarily became assimilated into the new culture. There was no choice, there was no option. For normal survival, that person had to learn the local language, associate with those already there, evolve into local religious expectations, and offer something to participate in maintaining the survival of that community. In effect, that person or family had to assimilate into the culture to survive.

This explains part of the answer to the demise of the Roman Empire.

Roman soldiers located far from Rome and cut off from many of their fellow Romans often became assimilated into the local populations they controlled. Eventually, many Romans were Roman in name only. The Roman Empire finally collapsed when they didn't have funds to maintain the Roman identity and dominance throughout the Empire. This is partially a lesson, in reverse, as to what happened in modern America.

To come to America in the early 1900s was a life-changing event for those new immigrants. They came to America because they wanted something better for themselves and their families. They wanted freedom to find themselves and explore their capabilities; they wanted an opportunity to expand their horizons; they wanted to experience the dream that any industrious person seeks. America was the place to find those things. They didn't come to America to change America. They only wanted to experience it. Today, however, technology and advanced communications have changed how a new immigrant looks at America.

Today, America is no longer a melting pot for immigrants. Advanced technology and communications allow them to segregate themselves into groups that maintain their individual morals, customs, and traditions of their home countries or within the localized groups within the United States. They can become a citizen of the United States without having to really assimilate into the culture and values of a traditional United States citizen. In America we have many citizens who call themselves American who are not really American, not the traditional American of American cultures and values.

America is no longer a melting pot. America is now many countries within a country. America is now guided by many religions that rip each other asunder. America is now ripped apart by those focused only on their own desires, such as gays and lesbians, who disregard the fabric of our culture that has long kept us all on a unified course toward country and God. America is now influenced by rampant and careless sexual behavior by those who demand society pay for contraception to support their folly.

We no longer share a fundamental foundation that requires togetherness. Now we have many foundations each in its own unique way that continue to rip America apart. All those separate and selfish ideologies came together on November 6, 2012 to kill the great American dream. Each of those small parts of America won their prize, but lost the greater dream in doing so. Those freedoms offered by a country formed and guided by the hand of God will soon be removed. They looked at little things and disregarded the most important - freedom and opportunity by the Grace of God. How did it happen? What are the seemingly little things that broke apart - killed - the hopes of a once great nation?

It was the votes from fragmented America, the different parts of America that didn't share America's traditional culture and values, that elected Barack Obama to a second term. Those votes reinforced and institutionalized the basis of his proclamation, "America is no longer a Christian nation." His first election was based on hope for a better future for all. His re-election was based on the expression of who he really was and what he really represented. It was the first direct attack on Christianity by a president. It was the first openly-proclaimed attack on "One nation under God."

This next article from theconservativeinfo.com explains further. It's titled, 'War Against Christianity:'

"On the surface war seems like a harsh word to apply to what we are beginning to see more and more of in the press, on the news and in the courts. War is the attempt to destroy and subdue what one considers its enemy. This "war" is not being waged against any other religion. It seems like these groups that are waging this "war" are more than willing to embrace any other religion as long as it does not name the name of Christianity. Anything that bears the name of Christ or relates to Christ in any way is legal game for their attacks. I could go into detail about the attacks against the Ten Commandments, Christmas, manger scenes, and on and on and on.

The very real and present danger lies in greater agendas though. These groups that are attacking Christianity have a deeper and far more sinister reason for their attacks. One reason for these attacks is that Christianity is in direct opposition to the open sinfulness some people want America to embrace. As long as America stands on Judea/Christian law, groups like sodomite's and lesbians will not be free to spread their poison across America. Organizations like NAMBLA (North American Man Boy Love Association) will always have their hands tied from pursuing their perverse lifestyles of seducing children. Political organizations like socialist (they hate Christianity), Feminist (They see Christianity as constrictive), left wing Democrats (Christianity is a burden) and others for political reasons are in support of eliminating Christianity from America. Religious groups that do not embrace Christianity such as the occult (A vastly growing community), Wicca (A very strong witchcraft community), Atheism (disavow God's existence), Satanism (worshipers of Satan), secularist (man is his own deity), Islam (worshipers of Allah (they hate Christianity and refer to us as infidels and dogs)), and others too many to list in their total number, all feel like they are strong enough together to destroy Christianity in

America. Together and separately, these groups fight to chip away at Christian liberty, using liberal left wing sympathetic courts to advance their attacks. These people have a hatred for Christianity that is fueled by Satan himself. Every time a left wing judge who is sympathetic to them gets on the bench they get stronger.

The other focus is an idealistic and political desire to have the world come together in one mind and spirit of working together for what is called the betterment of all of mankind without God. These people see religion as the source of all the worlds evil. They blame most wars on religion and they are right. The problem is that they place true Christianity in this group and nothing could be further from the truth.

Perverted Christianity by people who have private agendas and an anti-Semitic mindset use Christianity to further their ends just like they use any convenient vessel to spread their hate. The people who believe this are blind to the truth and they do not want to see how Christianity has been used by corrupt people.   These groups believe man is his own God.

John Lennon who was a member of the communist party spoke of this in his song "Imagine". This song was written to promote a world without God, heaven or hell. This song could be an anthem for communism and people embraced the song like it was the greatest thing that ever came along. It received accolades for greatness and the song was a slap in the face to democracy and Christianity.

Some have called this mindset that is working to bring the world together in one accord "The one world order". Some of you will laugh at that. Laugh on, but read on please. Many of you have seen logos and different things at work depicting this mindset, even if you did not recognize it for what it was. The company I worked for had these. One was a screen saver they encouraged everyone to install on their company computers. They also have it in printed form that can be posted around the plant. It started out with the company logo in the center of the screen and then sentences began coming outward from the logo. These sentences were comprised of statements such as "One World", "One Team", "One Mind", "One Goal", "One Thought", "One Voice", etc. Christianity is the only religion in the world that distinctly teaches against and has dire warnings concerning this order.

Christianity relates this time to a world leader that will bring the entire world together for a brief time in a peace and prosperity like the world has never seen. This leader will be hailed as the true Messiah. All of the world will flock to his banner. This peace will only be a short lived one though. His leadership will usher in a time of violence and war like the world has never seen.

This makes Christianity a direct opposing force to the completion of these groups' goals for a world united together for the benefit of all mankind as one people. These left wing groups are activists working toward this goal. On the surface this seems like a wonderful idea. Who would not want the world to come together working together with one mind and one goal. There are far too many reasons to go into in this article why this will not work according to Christianity. Christian ministers have been preaching about this world order and the reasons it will not work for centuries. The Bible has a lot to say about this time called "the end times".

These left wing activist do want a financially strong America and a unified America, just not a conservative or a conservative Christian

America. For years now, these left wing groups have been wanting to destroy anything that strengthens America and unifies us as a conservative or a Christian nation. They have attacked relentlessly everyone from Columbus to the founding fathers to any other person or event that traditional Americans admire and look up to.

They have tried to change history concerning the siege of the Alamo. They have tried to show the founding fathers in a cruel and vicious light. They make sure they remind you that Thomas Jefferson owned slaves and had children by them. They do not tell you that it was the accepted norm of the time. It is just a way they throw dirt at the founding fathers.

This traditional mindset which is grounded in Christianity must be destroyed before the United States will be open minded enough to be a true member of a "One Mind, One World, One Team, One Thought", One Voice" order.

These same people recently tried to smear and ridicule a great American president (Ronald Reagan). They know they cannot reach the older Americans who have been brought up in patriotic pride. They want to infiltrate the education system, courts and media to supplant their Christian morality and traditions in what has made America the light and strength of freedom for all the world to see.

They have a hatred for the grass roots traditions that made America great that burns with an unquenchable fire. This same fire of hatred is what makes them hate George W. Bush like they do. They see their agendas set back with every day that he spends in the White House and they are like ravenous dogs in their unrelenting and deceitful attacks against him. I believe their hatred is so strong they would even challenge the Constitution itself to get him out of office. I hear some of these left wing liberal Bush haters on TV and I (God forbid) get the idea sometimes that they are anxiously waiting to see another attack against America by terrorist so it will give them ammunition to use against him. Television cannot hide the fire of hatred that you can see in their eyes when they speak about him.

They have a burning hatred for Christian morality and traditions that has made America the light and strength of freedom. They want an America that is free from conservative tradition. They want an America where sin is not defined by Christian morality. They want an America free from restraints upon their actions. They want an America not hobbled by Christian codes of ethics. These groups want the rule of law to be "anything goes". They want an America that does not remind them that they have moral responsibility. These left wing groups feel like they have to break the hold Christianity has on America in order for their goals to be achieved.

Some of these left wing groups would embrace with enthusiasm an America more socialist in its politics and reforms. They want the people to depend on the government to supply peoples every need and want. This gives them power over the people. They do not want people to accept responsibility for their own actions or their future. They want the government to be the peoples security blanket against losing their lifestyle. If the people fall on hard times, they want a government that is there to tell them what went wrong and to bail them out. They want people to get so dependent on the government that they cry out like a spoiled child "I deserve better and you (the government) owe it to me". This puts the government in control and the people as dependents. The founding fathers had a different plan. Their plan was for the government to be controlled by and answerable to "We the people". Liberal left wing activist want to change that. They feel like they know what is best for the people. They want the people answerable to the government. I feel like they would change the Constitution from "We the people, in order to form a more perfect union", to read "We the government, in order to form a more perfect union."

Yes, there is a war against Christianity. There is a war against the grass roots traditions of our founding fathers. There is a war against an America governed by law founded on Christian morality and principles. There is a war against the family unit as defined by Christianity." End of article.

A last question we must ask about our security as American citizens: If God is removed from our military forces, who have sworn to God to protect us and our American values, who then is left to protect us? What will their actions be when forced with that final and important decision if and when directed by a tyrannical government to do otherwise? This book is dedicated to that question.

A War on Christians is a War Against America.

A War on Christians is a War Against God.
###

About the Author

Will Clark's author experiences began by writing inspection and evaluation reports in the U.S. Air Force. He is a retired Air Force officer and a Vietnam veteran, serving in Saigon from 1966 to 1967. His other overseas assignments include Misawa, Japan and Ankara, Turkey.

In 1995, he authored a book, *How to Learn*, as a county-wide study skills project to encourage students to improve their grades in DeSoto County, Mississippi. Education supporters printed and distributed four thousand copies. He also wrote a weekly education column for a local newspaper, *The Desoto County Tribune,* the following school year.

His next published book was *School Bells and Broken Tales*, a parody of nursery rhyme characters, also a motivation and education book for children. His other books include *Shades of Retribution*, a historical novel, and *Simply Success*, a motivation guide for students and employees.

His action novels include a trilogy based on Atlantis and crystals. The first book is titled: *The Atlantis Crystal.* The second book is titled: *She Waits In Atlantis.* The third is: *Return to Atlantis.* This trilogy is based on his travels while assigned to Turkey, site of the ancient city of Troy.

His previous political action novel, *666: Mark of the Beast*, is a sequel to another political action novel, *America 20XX: The New World Order.*

Clark and his wife, Marie, live in Diamondhead, Mississippi, where they play golf with many friends.

For more information about the author visit:

http://www.authorsden.com/visit/author.asp?authorid=1496

Things We Must Never Forget
Until We Know All the Answers

Benghazi

Why were four Americans killed?
Where was Hillary Clinton while it was happening?
Where was Barack Obama while it was happening?
Why did they lie and blame the event on a video?
Why were rescuers on 'stand by' told to 'stand down?'

Fast and Furious

Who authorized the operation?
Why did the operation continue after weapons were lost?
Why did the procedure have no procedure?
Why weren't tracking devices used?

The IRS Scandal

What was the highest level involved?
Who initiated it?
Why hasn't anyone been fired or reprimanded?
What dangers could be unleashed by this organization?

Greatest Quotes
of
Our Time

Michelle Obama
February 18, 2008
"For the first time in my adult life I am proud of my country."
(Age 44)

Barack Obama
March 9, 2008
"We are no longer a Christian nation - at least not just."

September 25, 2012
Remarks to the UN General Assembly
"The future must not belong to those who slander Islam."

Nancy Pelosi
March 9, 2010
"We have to pass the bill so that you can find out what is in it."

Hillary Clinton
January 23, 2013
"What difference, at this point, does it make?"

Other Books by the Author

Novels:
Shades of Retribution
The Atlantis Crystal
She Waits in Atlantis
Return to Atlantis
America 20XX: The New World Order
666: Mark of the Beast
Death Drones: 2025

Children's Books:
Forest Trails and Fairy Tales
Wishing Wells and Broken Tales
Student Study Skills
American Heroes: Students Who Learn

Non-Fiction:
Simply Success
The Education Jungle
How to Learn
The Day America Died
Obama's Ring: The Seat of Satan
Managing Without Conflict
The Peer Pressure Monster
Denied 3 Times